Acknowledgements

In addition to the authors named in the **List of Contributors** to this manual, Scottish Cycling acknowledges the following individuals and organisations for their part in developing this resource and supporting the work of the SMBLA.

Richard Arrowsmith, Lagganlia Outdoor Centre
Bridget Dales and Eleanor MacGregor, Scottish Natural Heritage
Gavin Howat, Health & Safety Executive
Bob Telfer, Adventure Activities Licensing Authority
All SMBLA Tutors

Scottish Advisory Panel for Outdoor Education
British Cycling
sportscotland
The Hub in the Forest, Glentress
Glenmore Lodge National Training Centre
www.fine-adc.co.uk

D0495867

Photography credits

Emma Guy
Graeme Herd
Ian Linton
Andy McCandlish
Richard Martin
Drew Michie
Claire Nicol
Ken Russell
Cliff Smith
Ewan Thomson
Nancy Thomson
Neil Walker
Jack Wardell
Cliff White
Gary Willis

Contents

Editors' Note

The publication of this manual has arisen largely in response to the phenomenal growth of the SMBLA Scheme since the first training courses were run in 1997. The content of the original training modules that formed the "home-produced" training manual which this publication replaces, has been revised and updated where necessary. Substantial revision has occurred for the Access section, for example, to take account of new legislation and official guidelines. Other sections have been added to provide more information on topics already included in the award syllabus (Bike Set-up, the Safe Cycle & Trailside repairs and Terrain & Route selection), or which have become more important issues for mountain bike leadership since the development of the Scheme (Hazards & Risk Management and Legal Issues & Liability). The theme of leadership remains primary throughout. However, the Manual now represents both a comprehensive training resource for leaders and a reference manual for any mountain biker, whether leading, being led, or operating alone.

Throughout the Manual some sections of text have been highlighted in blue; these represent information of particular importance for leaders to be aware of. The SMBLA logo has also been used to mark important points of information with respect to the Award Scheme, and to make the distinction between parts of the modules which apply specifically to one level of the Award: Trail Cycle Leader, Mountain Bike Leader or Expedition.

Scottish Cycling is committed to maintaining and improving the high standards of the SMBLA Awards and its resources. We would welcome any comments on the Manual or on any aspect of the Award Scheme. Please send your comments to: smbla@scottishcycling.com

Jenny Wright & Claire Nicol

FOREWORD

By Nigel Williams

 The development of mountain biking in general, and the use of the activity within outdoor education, has seen an extraordinary growth over the past five years. In order to manage this development professionally, Scottish Cycling developed the SMBLA Scheme, a universally approved award scheme, recognised throughout UK by a wide range of outdoor organisations, including AALA (Adventure Activities Licensing Authority), local authorities, mountain bike shops and centres, and even the military. The SMBLA awards have become the Industry Standard in off-road leadership qualifications.

In 1997 a small group of Scottish mountain bikers who were outdoor instructors in other activities such as skiing, kayaking, mountaineering and sailing got together to develop a syllabus for an award scheme that would meet the needs of outdoor education and the leisure industry. The SMBLA Scheme is currently the fastest growing sports award scheme in the UK, with over 1000 qualified trail cycle & mountain bike leaders in six years and a third of that figure in the last year, so it appears to be growing exponentially.

This publication provides the support and guidance for an enthusiastic association of Leaders working throughout the UK. It meets the need for a concise reference manual and training resource on coaching and group leadership for anyone leading or aspiring to lead groups biking off road. It is not just competitors who need coaching, in recreational or educational terms. Coaching and leadership interweave; good coaching is also good leadership and coaching good skills improves safety and enjoyment for the individual, which makes leading the group a more rewarding experience.

The contributors to this manual are a who's who of outdoor professionals with many years of experience and coaching in a wide variety of outdoor activities. Many of the ideas in this manual are transferable to, and from, other forms of outdoor activity. Hopefully this will encourage more outdoor leaders to join the qualification scheme and take these skills and knowledge to new heights as each generation learns from the previous one.

A resource like this does not come together easily. The whole team of contributors has achieved a remarkably high quality of material and it is hard to pick out anyone in particular. However, Jim Riach and Jenny Wright deserve high praise for managing the project, whilst simultaneously facilitating the rapid development of the award scheme. We are all indebted to your vision and enthusiasm which has driven the success of the Scheme and this manual to a reality.

Nigel Williams is Head of Training at Glenmore Lodge, near Aviemore, a National Training Centre of international repute in the field of outdoor skills and leadership training. He has been a strong supporter of the Scheme and has contributed his knowledge of the Mountain Leader Training schemes through his involvement with the Scottish and UK Mountain Leader Training Boards.

List of Contributors

John Cheesmond
John has a background in mountain instruction and was a key player in the development of ski leader qualifications during the eighties and early nineties. He enjoys mountain biking, though his main interest is now in cycle touring, both in Britain and Europe. He also participates in audax rides throughout Scotland, covering distances from 100km up to 600km.

John Fulton
John Fulton has been an SMBLA Tutor since 1998 and is Director of Wildcat Adventures. He has over 20 years leading mountain biking holidays in Europe, Asia, Middle East, and Morocco. John has competed in the Mountain Bike World Championships and British Championships. Formerly a Training Officer with the local Mountain Rescue Team, John has acquired a considerable amount of mountain experience both in Scotland and abroad, including 12 Alpine seasons.

Matt Healey
Matt is a Senior Instructor for the Outward Bound Trust based in the Lake District and holds professional qualifications in a variety of outdoor sports. He has been a committed mountain biker since 1987 and has been a Tutor for the SMBLA since 2001. He currently fulfills the role of Technical Advisor for the Outward Bound Trust under the terms of its Adventure Activities License and manages a wide range of adventurous personal development programs across the UK. He is also the Vice Chair for the Lake District Association of Mountain Bikers (LAMB) and represents the interests of the sport within the National Park in which he lives and works. He has competed in Trailquest and Polaris events and ridden recreationally all over the UK and Europe.

Greg Knowles
Greg is the manager of Dumfries and Galloway Council Outdoor Activity Service. He was involved in setting up the SMBLA Award Scheme. A regular bike rider, Greg also races both on road and of-road and has been involved in many other outdoor activities at various levels.

Peter Leach
Peter has spent his teaching career in Outdoor Education. He now cycles, runs and mountaineers recreationally and works as an ecologist specialising in amphibians and reptiles. He is also a first aid trainer.

Drew Michie
A former professional footballer, PE teacher and Outdoor Education Adviser with a Scottish local authority, Drew is one of the originators of the scheme. He has been involved in coach education since 1970, training and assessing kayak instructors. He also trains and assesses alpine ski leaders for Snowsport Scotland.

Claire Nicol
Claire Nicol joined Scottish Cycling in 2004 as Administrator. She has become closely involved with the SMBLA and brings her own experience

of mountain biking and working in outdoor and bike shops to the team.

Irene Riach
Irene qualified as an accredited sports dietitian in 1999 and has worked in sports nutrition ever since. Though she works full time for a premier league football team Irene has provided a sports nutrition service to a variety of sports during this time, including curling, athletics, badminton, swimming, triathlon, rugby and cycling. Irene attended the Commonwealth Games as a consultant Dietitian and she has traveled with both football and cycling nationally and internationally. She is an ISAK level 2 anthropometrist and is accredited with RESCU and the BOA. Irene is a keen mountain biker, cycle tourist, adventure racer and, more recently, a mum.

Jim Riach
Jim Riach is Education Officer for Cycling Scotland where he is responsible for a range of education and training courses. Formerly with Scottish Cyclists' Union, he is one of the founder members of the SMBLA and was instrumental in setting up the scheme and developing the course material. Jim is a British Cycling Coach Educator, an ABCC Senior Coach, a BC MTB A-Grade Commissaire, and has coached and officiated at club and international level. He is a member of the SRSC Safe Cycle Working Group and the Scottish Mountain Safety Forum. Jim was a competitive mountain biker, having raced in both domestic and international MTB cross-country races and has ridden recreationally in Europe and America.

Cliff Smith
Cliff Smith is Outdoor Education Development Officer for the City of Edinburgh Council. He holds a number of high level outdoor qualifications in mountaineering, kayaking, canoeing and mountain biking. He has a keen interest in long, self sufficient off-road mountain bike trips and got involved with the SMBLA to develop this part of the scheme. When not working in the great outdoors, his main passions are running marathons and paragliding. An unfulfilled ambition is to combine a mountain bike expedition with some paragliding...one day!

Cliff White
Cliff White is a SMBLA tutor with many years experience teaching outdoor education in secondary schools. He is active in Edinburgh RC, one of the foremost cycling clubs in the UK, and is organiser of the Glentress Trailquest.

Nigel Williams
Nigel Williams is Head of Training at Glenmore Lodge. He has been a strong supporter of the SMBLA awards and has contributed his knowledge of the Mountain Training schemes through his involvement with the Scottish and UK Mountain Leader Training Boards.

Jenny Wright
Jenny Wright is lead Administrator with Scottish Cycling and currently SMBLA Secretary. She has a PhD in plant ecology, for which she which undertook field research in Scotland and Scandinavia. Formerly a keen hill walker, she maintains a keen interest in the Scottish countryside. While now competing on road and track, she came into the sport through mountain biking. Jenny is also a British Cycling Club Coach.

Introduction

ORIGINS OF THE SMBLA SCHEME
The Scottish Mountain Bike Leader Scheme was developed by **Scottish Cycling** (SC) in conjunction with the **Scottish Advisory Panel for Outdoor Education** (SAPOE) in order to provide a framework and qualification for Leaders to deliver mountain biking as a safe and enjoyable sport and activity which would satisfy the needs of Local Authorities and the Adventure Activities Act.

It was recognised that while the governing bodies of cycle sport had a well established coaching structure aimed at improving competitive performance, they were not addressing the need for personnel with leadership competence who could facilitate non-competitive experience of the sport for groups of people of wide ranging abilities and aspirations. It was with this dual aim in mind, to develop a leadership qualification, and to encourage participation in mountain biking through group-led activities, that the SMBLA Scheme was founded.

In 1997 the first Tutors were trained and pilot courses run to develop the Scheme's two levels of award. Also in this year, the Scottish Mountain Bike Leader Association (SMBLA) was formed by Scottish Cycling in order to manage the awards and related issues.

SC and SAPOE bring together a broad base of expertise across recreational and competitive mountain biking as well as outdoor activities and leadership schemes in other sports and education.

Scottish Cycling, the governing body for cycle-sport in Scotland and an integral part of British Cycling, is the administrative and awarding body for all SMBLA qualifications.

SMBLA ENDORSEMENT

The SMBLA scheme is endorsed by the **Adventure Activities Licensing Authority** (AALA) and **Mountain Leader Training Scotland** (MLTS), and recognised by **British Cycling** (BC), the governing body for cycle-sport in Great Britain. Her Majesty's Forces is also endorsing the Scheme, with all RAF recruits undertaking the award. In the near future all Joint Services Adventure Training Instructors (JSATI) will be qualified SMBLA leaders.

There are several other off-road cycle training organisations in the UK which operate as commercial training providers. However, the SMBLA Scheme is the only award scheme where the national governing body is responsible for both the administration and awarding functions.

SMBLA TUTORS

All SMBLA Tutors are registered with Scottish Cycling and provide TCL, MBL and Expedition courses on behalf of Scottish Cycling. Tutors may be employed by a local authority or by an outdoor education provider, or they

may work independently, but they all operate to the same guidelines agreed by the awarding body, and they all deliver the same syllabus.

During their qualification, SMBLA Tutors undertake the Sports Coach UK Coach Educator course, and become competent as a Tutor through an apprenticeship period taking approximately 12 months of observing, assisting and being assessed by experienced, qualified SMBLA Tutors. Most SMBLA Tutors hold equivalent qualifications in other outdoor activities such as canoeing, mountaineering, skiing and climbing.

A full list of qualified Tutors is available from the Scottish Cycling website www.scottishcycling.com or by contacting the Scottish Cycling office.

STRUCTURE OF THE SMBLA AWARDS

The SMBLA scheme provides **training** and **assessment** in mountain biking and leadership skills and offers awards at two levels in progression:

Level 1: The **Trail Cycle Leader** Award (TCL) consists of a 2-day training course followed by a 1-day assessment, for use in AALA defined non-licensable terrain which covers:

✓ public highways, way marked routes, rights of way on which cycles are permitted, identifiable routes, tracks and trails with obvious navigational features and **routes with low to medium technical difficulty**
✓ routes which are 90-95% rideable over their total length

- ✓ terrain **no more than 30 minutes walk away from a shelter with communication** and **no more than 600 metres in height**
- ✓ normal summer conditions, **during daylight** *
- ✓ multi-day trips where the group does not require to be self sufficient

Level 2: The **Mountain Bike Leader** Award (MBL) consists of an additional two days training plus a 1-day assessment, for use in AALA defined licensable terrain which covers:

- ✓ public highways, way marked routes, rights, of way on which cycles are permitted, identifiable routes, tracks and trails with obvious navigational features and **routes of considerable technical difficulty**
- ✓ routes which are 90-95% rideable over their total length
- ✓ terrain **more than 30 minutes walk from the nearest shelter with communication** (AALA defined licensable terrain)
- ✓ any height above sea level
- ✓ normal summer conditions, **during daylight** *
- ✓ multi-day trips where the group does not require to be self sufficient

An additional **Expedition Endorsement** is available to both TCL and MBL holders, and consists of a 2-day combined training and assessment course. An **expedition** is defined as a trip of one or more nights where the group is entirely **self-sufficient**

*Note on night riding
Neither TCL nor MBL training currently covers night riding. Although being prepared for riding in fading light or poor daylight conditions is included within the syllabus, a TCL or MBL is not qualified to lead a group in full darkness, even with adequate lighting. The SMBLA recognises that night riding is an attractive and often realistic option for many mountain bikers, especially on short winter days. However, there are significantly greater risk factors attached to night riding, not least difficulties in navigation and group management. An additional module in night riding may be developed in the future.

SMBLA CANDIDATE PATHWAY
The candidate pathway of the SMBLA awards is similar to that of the Mountain Leader Award. Candidates must be over 18 in order to comply with legislation and insurance for leading groups in the outdoors.

Further information about the award scheme, including registration forms and a programme of courses, is available from the Scottish Cycling website (www.scottishcycling.com) or by contacting the office (Tel. 0131 652 0187).

Anyone wishing to qualify as a **Trail Cycle Leader** must progress through the following stages:

1. Register with the SMBLA (using the SMBLA Registration Form) to receive a registration number together with all course documentation. The Official Manual is a course requirement and can be purchased at the time of registration which can be done on-line through the Scottish Cycling website.

2. Complete the **SMBLA Logbook** (see Appendix) as evidence of mountain biking experience which is a pre-entry requirement for TCL training (see below)

3. Book and attend a 2-day **TCL training course.** Scottish Cycling's website has a list of courses, and details of SMBLA Tutors who may be contacted to arrange a course to suit.

4. Consolidate experience, taking into account Tutor feedback from the training course

5. Gain a valid **first aid qualification** (see below) which is a pre-requirement for TCL assessment

6. Have current **membership of Scottish Cycling / British Cycling** (see below)

7. Book and attend a **TCL assessment course** where you will be expected to be competent in all theoretical and practical aspects of the TCL syllabus

8. Successful candidates will receive a **TCL certificate** awarded by Scottish Cycling

A valid Trail Cycle Leader certificate is a pre-entry requirement for the next stage of the award, **Mountain Bike Leader**. The same stages 2-8 then apply for the MBL award.

LOGBOOK COMPLETION

A completed logbook detailing previous mountain bike experience and providing a referee is a pre-entry requirement for TCL and MBL training. Blank Logbooks (as shown in the Appendix) are provided on registration.

Logbook evidence should consist of at least 20 mountain bike rides of 1.5 hrs duration in a variety of weather conditions. Longer rides of 2-3 hrs duration, with at least one being 6 hours, and 2-3 detailed route cards should also be included. **The terrain covered should be appropriate to the level of award sought**. Rides may be undertaken in the UK or abroad.

FIRST AID QUALIFICATION

Prior to TCL assessment, and for any SMBLA award to remain valid, Leaders must hold an appropriate first aid qualification. Accepted first aid training courses should be provided by organisations approved by HSE for the purpose of first aid training, and delivered by staff who are registered with that organisation as first aid trainers or assessors. Courses must be a minimum of **12 hours**, with no sessions shorter than 2 hours.

First Aid Courses must include:

- action at an incident
- management of an unconscious casualty
- resuscitation
- treatment and control of bleeding
- treatment of injuries to bones, muscles and joints.
- recognition and treatment of shock
- treatment of choking
- recognition and treatment of common illnesses
- contents of first aid kits

The course must contain material relevant to the outdoor environment.

A list of approved first aid providers can be found in the Useful Contacts section.

SCOTTISH CYCLING / BRITISH CYCLING MEMBERSHIP

Prior to TCL assessment all candidates must be members of Scottish Cycling / British Cycling. Membership applications should be sent to the Scottish Cycling office. Members will receive a membership card which has a 6-digit membership number, and is valid for 12 months from the date of issue. Your card will show "**Scottish MTB Leaders**" as your membership grouping and you will be given the endorsement "Leader" by British Cycling at this stage. This card must be shown to the assessment Tutor. (Existing SC/BC members of a club or race team affiliated to SC/BC will have "SMBLA" added as their second claim club and should complete the relevant box in section 1 of the membership form).

There are three categories of SC/BC membership: Bronze, Silver and Gold. **Bronze** membership provides basic membership benefits, including a provisional racing licence, but no insurance cover to operate as a Leader. **Silver** and **Gold** membership provide **Third Party (Public Liability)** insurance and legal advice and assistance (to UK residents). **Gold** members are additionally entitled to Personal Accident insurance. **If you work freelance or are not covered by your employer's insurance, the Silver or Gold membership level is strongly recommended**.

Professional Indemnity insurance is available to all TCL and MBL holders who can present evidence of appropriate training in **Good Practice & Child Protection** at the time of membership application. Details of the insurance offered through membership are available from British Cycling.

TCL / MBL TRAINING COURSES

There are a maximum of 8 candidates on a TCL or MBL training course. Training courses normally takes place over two full days. The majority of courses are non-residential. A programme of "open" courses is available on the Scottish Cycling website. Course dates may also be arranged by contacting any of the SMBLA Tutors direct. Many Tutors are able to arrange courses on demand and tailor them to group requirements. Tutors will provide individual feedback in the form of an "Action Plan". This allows candidates to improve their knowledge and experience in areas wanting, in preparation for assessment.

All candidates must take to their training course:

1. Proof of SMBLA registration – a Registration letter issued by Scottish Cycling with a unique Registration number
2. Their SMBLA Course Manual which contains all the modules for TCL and MBL training

TCL / MBL ASSESSMENT

There are a maximum of 4 candidates on a TCL or MBL assessment. Assessment lasts one full day. Candidates who, on completion of a TCL/ MBL training course, are deemed competent in all areas by the Tutor may proceed straight to assessment.

All candidates must take to their assessment:

1. A "Training Completed" form issued by the Tutor after a training course
2. Their BC/SC membership card
3. A copy of their First Aid certificate
4. Their SMBLA Course Manual

 There is currently no automatic entry to TCL or MBL assessment through Accreditation of Prior Learning (APL), even though candidates may have considerable mountain bike experience and/or relevant teaching or leadership qualifications in other activities. Training with other off-road award schemes has proven not to meet the required standards of the SMBLA award, and does not guarantee candidates will meet the SMBLA assessment criteria.

VALIDITY OUTSIDE THE UK

The SMBLA awards are currently valid anywhere in the UK and Europe. Insurance to work as a Leader provided through Scottish Cycling / British Cycling membership extends to all European countries.

THE SMBLA AWARDS SYLLABUS

The following tables contain the syllabus for the Trail Cycle Leader and Mountain Bike Leader Awards, and the Expedition module which is available to both Trail Cycle Leaders and Mountain Bike Leaders. Tutors will take into account candidate experience and tailor courses accordingly. Candidates will be assessed on each of the Performance Criteria listed.

Performance Criteria for TCL Award

Log Book Experience / Evidence

At least 20 mountain bike rides in the log book of 1.5 h duration in appropriate terrain and in a variety of weather and conditions.

These should include longer rides (2-3 hrs) with at least one ride of 6h

The Safe Cycle

Can carry out a check on the bike and advise remedial action

Can make adjustments to brakes, gears, headsets and other components to make the bike safe

Demonstrates an understanding of how to set up an optimum riding position for the candidate

Clothing and Equipment

Attends with a bike, helmet and equipment suitable for the task and wearing appropriate clothing for a leader as a role model

Is able to advise on bikes and accessories suitable for the task

Can advise on appropriate clothing and safety equipment (gloves, glasses, helmets, footwear) for trail cycling

Fitness, Fuel & Hydration

Is physically fit enough to lead trail cycling activities for a range of groups

Appears adequately fuelled and hydrated and has available sufficient food/fluids to contend with a day's outing in TCL terrain and have energy in reserve

Shows an understanding of the fact that cycling is principally an endurance activity

Has a basic awareness of the major food groups and the refuelling requirements / limiting factors in endurance activity

Introductory Skills

Understands and can demonstrate the basic skills of cycling: setting off, braking, use of gears, cadence, hand position, covering brakes, balance

Techniques

Understands and can demonstrate the basic skills and techniques associated with trail cycling, including:

Front wheel lift, drop-off, 5 second balance, unweighting, climbing and descending

Managing a group

Can demonstrate responsible, effective and safe management of a group:
1. On-road
2. Off-Road

Shows an understanding of child protection and good practice issues

Trailside Repairs

Can effect most common repairs to enable a bike to be ridden back to base, including: puncture repair, broken chain, setting gear-stop screws, using knowledge and possession of appropriate tools

Shows awareness of potential wear and tear on equipment and knows how to minimise this

Leadership

Understands, accepts and can demonstrate a range of techniques involved in leading a trail cycle group

Uses appropriate tone, manner, pace and style

Is aware of and is able to use the action-centred leadership model – "team, task and individual"

Navigation

Is able to identify location at all times to within 100 metres using a map, compass and cycle computer

Demonstrates the use of these common navigational aids, along with guidebooks and route cards to plan and execute a flowing journey

Be able to accurately determine length and time for a route or leg

Planning and Preparation - the perfect trail cycling day.

Has an understanding of where to obtain an up to date weather forecast for the area, and the affect of different weather conditions on the group

Have in place "Late Back Procedures"

Have relevant knowledge of group qualities and competences, including medical history, parental consent and emergency contact number

Dealing with Emergencies

Be able to carry out a risk assessment of the planned activity

Understand and demonstrate the techniques used to deal with an emergency

Show an awareness of the shortcomings of the techniques

Countryside Awareness

Is aware of the current access legislation and where to get information both locally and nationally

Is able to identify routes suitable for trail cycling, and knows where to source this information

Has basic knowledge of various land use / management practices and how these affect mountain bikers, and understands the impact that mountain biking has on the environment

Cycle-Sport

Knows how to source information on cycling clubs and events

Is able to describe the differences between downhill and cross-country mountain bike events

Can describe how to run a simple cross-country event for novices

Performance Criteria for MBL Award

Log Book Experience/Evidence
At least 40 mountain bike trips in the log book

At least 10 rides must cover routes of extended length (6 hrs riding) and another 10 must cover routes with a high degree of technical difficulty, with at least 3 in remote terrain

At least 12 of these trips should have been as leader or assistant group leader

Skills
Must be able to climb and descend steep tracks and ride routes of a high degree of technical difficulty in comfort and style

Can perform bunny hop, lateral jump, wheelies, track stand, drop-offs, slow speed balance, corner at speed

Teaching
Be able to teach mountain bike skills as detailed above

Can prepare a basic lesson plan to teach the above

Is able to coach novice and intermediate cyclists and produce an improvement in their skill levels

Must show good ability in observation, performance analysis, and feedback

Can demonstrate a range of teaching styles and show an understanding of when these would be appropriate

Clothing and Equipment
Can advise on technical clothing and safety equipment (gloves, glasses, helmets, body armour)

Be able to give advice on bikes and accessories suitable for the task.

Understands the differences between specialist downhill and cross-country bikes

Attends with a bike and equipment suitable for the task and wearing appropriate clothing and footwear for a leader as a role model

Fitness, Fuel & Hydration
Is physically fit enough to lead mountain bike activities for a range of groups.

Appears adequately fuelled and hydrated and carries sufficient food/fluids to maintain energy levels

Is able to contend with a day's outing in MBL terrain and have energy in reserve

Shows an understanding of the fitness demands made by a variety of terrain

Can lead or contribute to a discussion on fuelling and hydration and their effects on health and performance

Multi Day Trips
Understands and can demonstrate the additional equipment and planning required to undertake multi-day trips (that do not fall within the scope of Expedition endorsement)

Shows an understanding of the variety of accommodation available to support such a trip

Range of Knowledge and Experience
Must show evidence of a sufficiently wide range of experience in mountain biking such that: the candidate would be:

- able to manage less experienced trail cycle leaders
- a credible and effective manager of mountain biking activities for other leaders or agencies
-

Managing a group
Can demonstrate responsible, effective and safe management of a group:

1. On-road
2. Off-Road in a remote environment

Trailside Repairs
Can effect most common repairs to enable a bike to be ridden back to base, e.g. broken pedal, bent wheel, broken spoke, damaged seat post, faults with disc brakes, including hydraulic brakes

Understands how the degree of expertise in trailside repairs of the leader will have an effect on the style of riding that can be permitted in more remote environments

Can either demonstrate or lead a discussion on more advanced trailside repairs

Leadership & Style
Understands, accepts and can demonstrate a range of techniques involved in leading a mountain bike group

Uses appropriate tone, manner, pace and style

Demonstrates a range of leadership styles

Aware of some more sophisticated theoretical models of leadership

Navigation
Be able to identify the group's location at all times to within 100 metres, using a map, compass and cycle computer

Can demonstrate the use of these common navigational aids in a remote environment

Be able to accurately determine length and time for a route or leg and deliver a flowing journey

Be able to demonstrate timing and pacing on foot. Have knowledge of Naismith's rule or equivalent

Planning and Preparation - The perfect mountain bike day
Have a good knowledge of weather and its effect on a group

Be able to interpret a variety of weather charts

Have in place "Late Back Procedures"

Be able to demonstrate techniques used to deal with a variety of water hazards

Have relevant knowledge of group qualities and competencies including:- medical history, parental consent and emergency contact numbers

Dealing with Emergencies
Be able to carry out a risk assessment of the planned activity

Understand and demonstrate the techniques used to deal with an emergency in a remote environment

Show an awareness of the shortcomings of the technique

Countryside Awareness
Be aware of the current access legislation and where to get information both locally and nationally. Knowledge of the Scottish Outdoor Access Code and Local Access Forum

Be able to identify routes suitable for mountain biking, and where to source this information

Have a good knowledge of the local environment that might include flora and fauna and environmental processes

Have a good knowledge of various land use/management practices and how these affect mountain bikers

Understand the impact that mountain biking has on the environment

Cycle-Sport
Have a knowledge of the various off-road disciplines and be able to describe downhill, cross-country, trailquest (cycle-orienteering) and 4-cross competitions

Know where to source up to date information on these disciplines

Performance Criteria for Expedition Module

Bike Set Up
Produce a bike in good mechanical order and fitted out for expeditioning

Be able to advise on bikes and fixtures suitable for the task

Show that equipment will be safely and securely carried in the main on the bike, or on a bike trailer

Clothing and Equipment
Be suitably dressed and have clothes to hand for all conditions likely to be encountered

Be able to advise on technical clothing and safety equipment (gloves, glasses, helmets)

Carry equipment in such a way that all essential items are in waterproof covers so that they are dry when needed

Expedition Trips
Understands and can demonstrate the additional equipment and planning required to undertake self-supporting expedition trip

Techniques
Understands and can demonstrate the basic skills and techniques associated with riding a loaded mountain bike

Shows an awareness of the differences between loaded and unloaded bikes

Managing a group
Can demonstrate responsible, effective and safe management of a group, off-road in a remote environment

Know how to prepare a group for a mountain bike expedition

Trailside Repairs
Carry appropriate expedition tools and repair kit, to include such extras as spare tyres, tools to tighten bottom brackets etc.

Be able to effect advanced trail side repairs to "get you home" e.g., buckled wheels, broken rear derailleur

Camp craft
Show good camp-craft skills including:

- ability to choose a good campsite
- ability to pitch a tent securely and quickly
- awareness of considerations of hygiene, and toilet arrangements around the campsite

Have knowledge of safety and environmental considerations, especially with regard to cooking around tents

Have knowledge of the different types of tents, stoves, sleeping bags etc and their advantages and disadvantages

Navigation
Be able to identify location at all times to within 100 metres, using a map, compass and cycle computer

Demonstrate the use of these common navigational aids in a remote environment

Be able to accurately determine length and trip time for a route or leg and deliver a flowing journey

Be able to demonstrate timing and pacing on foot

Planning and Preparation - The perfect mountain bike expedition

In addition to the above the Expedition Leader must show an ability to plan and prepare a group for a mountain bike expedition

Show good knowledge of weather and its effect on a group

Be able to interpret a variety of weather charts. Show an ability to interpret obvious weather patterns in the field

Have in Place "Late Back Procedures"

Be able to demonstrate techniques used to deal with a variety of water hazards

Have relevant knowledge of group qualities and competence including:- medical history, parental consent, emergency contact numbers

Dealing with Emergencies
Be able to carry out a risk assessment of the planned activity

Understand and demonstrate the techniques used to deal with an emergency in a remote environment

Show consideration of contingency plans and escape routes for when things go wrong

Have knowledge of the uses and limitations of mobile phones and radios on mountain bike expeditions

Show an awareness of the shortcomings of above the techniques

Countryside Awareness
Has awareness of the current access legislation and where to get information both locally and nationally

Show a knowledge of the Scottish Outdoor Access Code when sharing the countryside with other users

Have a basic background knowledge of the natural history, history, geology and geography of the area being used, and show evidence that they can communicate this knowledge to other people

Show an understanding of the impact that mountain biking has on the environment

Lecture Topic/Planning
Deliver a ten minute talk on a topic allocated by the Tutor

Produce suitable route plans / route cards for the expedition

Core Skills & Techniques

By the end of this section Leaders should be able to:-

- Describe the senses used by the mountain biker

- Describe the core skills and techniques of mountain biking

- List and demonstrate the main components of these skills and techniques

INTRODUCTION

The most challenging part of mountain biking is developing skills to deal with the huge variety of obstacles encountered out on the trails. Overcoming most of these obstacles requires linking only a few basic moves. It can seem complex negotiating a series of obstacles, but after breaking down and practising the basic moves, then putting it all together, it becomes instinctive.

It makes sense to start out on simple terrain, learning the basic moves, before moving up the skill ladder. This helps avoid frustration and creating physical and mental barriers to progress. Many of the skills can be developed at slow speed on artificial skill courses and transferred into "real live" or high speed skills out on the trail. Having competence and confidence at low speed often makes the skill happen naturally at higher speeds.

THE BASIC SKILLS

The basic skills have been broken down into seven groups or headings and are the skills that will be used even on the easiest of trails. **Proficiency in these basic skills is common to both the Trail Cycle Leader and Mountain Bike Leader awards.**

1. the neutral position
2. braking
3. gear selection
4. steering and cornering
5. fore and aft movements
6. choosing a line
7. climbing
8. descending

Before looking at these skills we will look at the senses that control the skills.

THE SENSES
Mountain biking relies heavily on the senses, particularly vision, touch and hearing, providing vital feedback to help develop riding skills.

Vision
The most important sense to the mountain biker, the position of the head and direction of vision determines the direction of travel. In other words, you go where you look. This means that the best way to avoid the big rock in the middle of the trail is to look past it. Keep your head up and continually scan the trail in front to see what's ahead. In non-technical sections your eyes should be focused between 3 and 15 metres in front of you. Don't stare at your front wheel or watch the rocks go by.

Touch
On a mountain bike touch or "tactile feedback" comes through your hands, backside and feet. It is this sensory feedback that keeps you in control of the bike. Beginners and out of control riders experience this feedback as if they were on top of a bucking stallion. More experienced riders become smooth and "light" on the bike, because they are moving with the bike rather than hanging on. Moving with the bike translates into making frequent adjustments (fore and aft, side to side, and up and down). When your timing is off, tactile feed back in the form of bumps and jolts will soon let you know it is time to take corrective action. If you momentarily lose your rhythm your elbows and knees can absorb some pretty big hits, *however your rear end cannot*. Big jolts through the saddle transmit too much shock to the spine. The best way to avoid this is to stand up when the going gets rough

Hearing
This may be the least important of the senses used in mountain biking but it is none the less important. The sound of your tyres provides feedback on the type of surface, from a low hum on tarmac to the warning sounds that loose gravel makes. You also need to know how to respond to your bike when it starts making unusual noises. The noises could just be annoying, like a misaligned derailleur, or small twigs caught in your wheel, but they could indicate something seriously wrong like the hiss of a puncture.

THE BASIC RIDING SKILLS

1. The Neutral position
This is the "ready" position in mountain biking and can be either seated or standing. Mountain bikers move all over the bike as the terrain changes and need to adopt a versatile position to allow these moves to take place smoothly. In the seated position the rider will have relaxed shoulders, elbows and knees. In the standing position the shoulders, elbows and knees remain relaxed allowing the body to act as a giant shock absorber, while the bike moves around beneath the rider. The pedals and feet are horizontal if not pedalling, and this forms a stable platform to stand and balance on. The saddle is principally an aid to balance with most of the weight bearing through the feet and legs.

2. Braking

This is a skill that is often overlooked or assumed. Anticipation and looking ahead to see what obstacles are coming up are the key to a smooth and enjoyable journey. Effective braking and the anticipation required for braking and gear changing are similar. Disc brakes are now standard on many mountain bikes and are even more powerful than rim brakes. Brake control skills should be practised on a gentle slope until a "sensitive touch" is developed. You can progress from gentle or planned braking (feathering) to the emergency stop.

Braking requires good anticipation to keep the bike under control. Much of the skill in braking is developing a "feel" for your bike and tuning in to the feedback coming through your feet, hands and your other senses. The pressure should be enough to slow the bike but not enough to make it skid. Once the wheels are skidding the effectiveness of braking is reduced. If the wheels start to lock the brakes can be modulated, i.e. pressure is released and then reapplied. Rear wheel skids can usually be controlled; front wheel skids are less predictable and are to be avoided at all costs. Skidding is not only less efficient but causes trail damage, wears out tyres and should be discouraged.

The front brake stops the bike fast, giving you roughly 70% of your braking power. If used violently it will have the effect of a catapult, launching you over the handlebars. The trail conditions also affect the effectiveness of the braking manoeuvre, and practice is required under different conditions. Wet rims increase stopping distance; water can be removed from wet rims by light application of the brakes prior to planned braking.

Emergency or severe braking, where you are fighting physics and the forces of nature, requires greater attention to body positioning and timing to perform this technique successfully. *Before* applying the brakes the rider should get as low and far back on the bike as possible, with the stomach close to the saddle and the chest low. The front brake should be applied smoothly, gradually increasing the pressure. The back brake increases the braking power and attempts should be made to minimise or stop skidding. Keeping your weight back keeps the rear end of the bike on the ground.

3. Gear Changing

Maintaining a smooth cadence (pedal rate) over varied terrain can help reduce fatigue. Maintaining that cadence requires frequent gear changes on variable/undulating terrain. Don't be afraid to use the full range of gears on your bike.

The majority of gear shifters on mountain bikes will now be either trigger shifters or twist grips. The left hand shifter operates the front derailleur and the right hand shifter operates the rear derailleur, and they usually operate index gear systems where one click means changing up or down one gear.

The concept of *"spinning"* is encouraged. This means pedalling at a reasonably high rate of 75-100 rpm (revolutions or pedal strokes per minute) which requires a low pedal force and allows the rider to stay aerobic and fresh for longer.

Going uphill requires a lower gear to maintain this cadence. This does not always require a shift from the front derailleur, but will require a downshift at the rear (note that a downshift at the rear actually sends the chain 'up' to a larger sprocket, which gives a lower gear).

Going downhill or riding with a tailwind may require an upshift at the rear (down to a smaller sprocket) and may mean an upshift at the front onto a larger chain ring.

After some practise little thought should be needed for gear changing, with leg speed the deciding factor. Gear changing can be made smoother and quicker by easing back on the power and soft pedalling as you shift. Though the gears will change under full power, easing back can make for faster and smoother changes and is kinder on componentry.

Although mountain bikes may have up to 27 gears there are some gear combinations that should be avoided to prevent damage to the chain:

the small chain ring at the front and the small sprocket at the rear

the large chain ring at the front and the large sprocket at the rear

These combinations put a sideways stress on the chain and may even snap it, it is sometimes referred to as *cross gearing*. There are no cross gears in the middle ring, so novice riders may find operating in the middle ring gives them sufficient gears for introductory rides.

4. Steering and Cornering
These are two closely linked techniques that have differences between the slow and the medium-fast techniques involved. At low speeds steering by turning the handlebars is used on technical sections to make the bike go where you want it to and in effect make it turn the corner. On a bike with some momentum, cornering is affected by leaning the bike, (not the body). Cornering can be made easier by putting weight on the inside handlebar and outside pedal. Leaning forward puts more weight on the front wheel and helps improve traction. To understand this concept try walking beside your bike while

holding only onto the saddle. When the bike is upright it travels in a straight line. Lean the bike toward you, and the front wheel turns and the rear follows, lean away and the same thing happens in the opposite direction.

Good steering technique can make the bike corner like it is on rails: by steering into medium and high speed corners more speed can be maintained whilst still turning tightly. Steering at speed originates from the knees and hips. The knees and hips move and point into the turn, with most of the weight on the outside pedal. The position is very similar to that of a skier carving a turn. In most situations you don't turn the front wheel but you lean the bike into the turn. The upper body remains square and the arms can be used to counter-steer, i.e. pull up with the outside arm and push down with the inside arm, to increase the steering effect.

5. Fore and Aft Movements

Balancing on a moving mountain bike is a complex skill that requires constant shifts of your body back and forth so that your weight stays centred over the bike. These moves help the bike flow over the terrain making the ride smoother, less tiring and more energy efficient. At times it is desirable to throw your weight off-centre to un-weight either of the wheels to make it easier to negotiate an obstacle. To get the fore-aft movement, start by adopting the neutral position, making sure that the knees and elbows are flexed and springy. Move slowly forward by placing a lot of weight on your hands, then move back so that your hips are behind the seat feeling the transfer of weight to the rear wheel. Once you have the feel for these movements, try lifting the front wheel from a variety of positions to see what effect your body position has on this action.

6. Choosing a line

Depending on where you cycle the terrain can vary greatly. For example, opposite sides of a hill or valley can have different ground conditions due to the type of soil, vegetation, slope and drainage. Trails can vary in an instant from smooth fire road, to rocks and roots, mud and water, and even sand. Knowing what happens to the bike on these surfaces is important.

Begin by linking the terrain and hazards in an area you know well and finding out the best lines. This experience can then be used on new trails allowing you to anticipate the hazards in different types of terrain.

According to professional mountain bikers, "the line is everything". The challenge is to find the best line to get you through that section. It will vary according to the surface and whether you are ascending or descending. Anticipating the affect that natural hazards will have on the handling of the bike is the key to an enjoyable and successful mountain bike ride.

The tips on the following page will get you started:

Rocks and roots

For rocks it is best to stand up and let the bike move underneath you. Tree roots can be similar to rocks and should be approached as close to 90° as possible; both can be extremely slippery when wet and should be treated with care.

Mud

Mud is likely to be encountered on any UK trail, even in summer. You should move your weight back to counteract the braking effect. You need to try and stay light and keep pedalling. If you do come to a standstill try heaving the bike forwards by throwing your weight forwards.

Water

Water should be tackled at low speed; underlying rocks can be slippery, and muddy water can conceal big holes and rocks. Dark, murky pools should be avoided.

Sand

Sand, which is often associated with water, has the ability to sap your energy and usually needs speed to negotiate it. You should be careful however, as sand can throw your steering out very quickly.

Picking a line and sticking to it can be difficult, especially on single track. Good riders and racers "visualize" their way down the trail. You can try this technique by stopping at the beginning of a section, picking out the line you want to take, and building a mental picture or map of the section. You then ride it looking at that line, the one in your mental map. Let your bike follow your eyes, look where  you want to go. Don't look where you don't want to go because that is where you will end up.

7. Climbing

To experience the exhilaration of descending, you first have to climb to the top! Before climbing select the right gear; it is much more difficult to change gear when you are already climbing, especially if you are over-geared. (See section on gear changing).

On long climbs stay in the saddle and move your weight back to keep traction. You are likely to need to counter-balance any front wheel lift, by taking the weight of your upper body forward and leaning low onto the handlebars. Develop a rhythm on the long climbs by counting 1- 2- 3, pushing a little harder every third stroke. Use good pedalling technique by pedalling in a circle if you have toe straps or clipless pedals, this allows you to pull-up as well as push down.

On short "power climbs", getting up out of the saddle and powering over them should allow you to maintain momentum. Once up out of the saddle you must adjust your weight to maintain traction on the rear wheel. In all climbing positions your grip on the handlebars should remain light to allow for small steering adjustments.

8. Descending
The hard work over, it is time for the exhilarating bit, the downhill. As you approach the descent make sure that you are in control of your speed and get ready to move your weight back over the back wheel. You should also put your bike into a gear that reduces chain-slap (i.e. middle to large chain ring at the front and middle to large sprocket at the rear).

On the descent keep two fingers over each brake lever so that you remain in control of your speed. Your legs and arms act as suspension, with the pedals level and a wide hand grip, giving you more control and feel for a good line choice. Most of your weight is on your feet, with the pedals horizontal or at the "quarter to three" position, ready to pedal when appropriate or necessary. A firm but relaxed grip is used on the handlebars and the majority of your weight is transferred to your feet. A standing position is adopted, allowing easy changes of position and reducing the amount of shock transferred to your spine.

The general rule of thumb is: sit down on the climbs, stand up on the descents. However, the design of some full suspension bikes means that this rule doesn't always apply.

The effect of slope steepness on the centre of gravity when riding downhill

The vertical arrows which run through the centre of the front and rear wheels represent gravity acting downwards.

The centre of gravity (X) is the midpoint between the two arrows.

When descending, a rider must keep his weight as close to the centre of gravity as possible.

As the slope becomes steeper the distance between the arrows becomes less, and the centre of gravity shifts towards the rear of the bike.

The rider must correspondingly shift his body weight backwards to maintain balance and traction.

The margin for error is less as the slope becomes steeper, demanding correct body positioning to maintain control.

1. Gentle slope

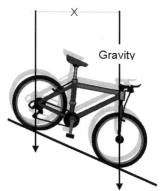

2. Moderate slope

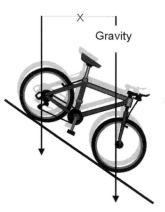

3. Steep slope

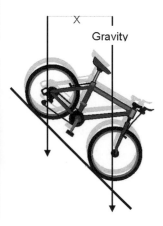

CORE TECHNIQUES

The core techniques combine many of the skills above into the common "moves" repeated again and again when out biking. **Refer to the syllabus for TCL and MBL (in the Introduction) for a list of the skills included in each level of the award. For the MBL award many of these techniques may be combined to form a skills test in the assessment.**

The 5-second Balance or Track Stand

Slow or zero speed skills help develop poise and balance on the bike and ultimately improve other skills that are done with some speed. Cycling requires good balance. Remember those early days of learning to ride a bike! Balance drills help develop this skill further.

Practising balance skills will reduce the panic zone before unclipping your feet from the pedals, and allows you to take the necessary amount of time to make a good choice of route or technique for particular obstacles. The track stand (so called because it is a skill employed by sprint cyclists on the track) is also a cool technique to use while stopped at traffic lights. Rock strewn,  gnarly sections are generally ridden at low speeds, and anyone without good balance skills will likely need to walk such sections. Practising the skills on steep ascents or descents help define the most effective body position for riding these sections.

Ratcheting

At some point you are sure to encounter a trail so festooned with rocks, roots and deep ruts that normal pedalling is impossible because your pedals, and cranks hit off these obstacles. You can keep your pedals and cranks clear of the obstacles by keeping the cranks more or less horizontal and pumping the pedals up and down. Combined with feathering of the brakes you should be able to ride over rocky/rooted sections without putting your feet down.

Canting

On uphill sections where ratcheting is impossible as you reach stall point, you can "cant" the bike on the downstroke of the pedal by leaning the bike to the side and gain a few extra inches of clearance for the pedals, chain ring and rear mech. In extreme situations it may allow you to limbo under low hanging branches. Combining these two techniques should allow you to deal with the gnarliest of terrain.

MBL

Front Wheel Lift

This is achieved by pulling up on the bars combined with a hard pedal stroke in a low gear lifting the front wheel onto the obstacle. The technique is used for riding over logs, "bumping" up onto a kerb and ascending a stepped climb. The front wheel lift is usually followed by a rear wheel lift to allow safe and gentle passage of the rear wheel over the obstacle. After the front wheel is raised, punch the bars forward to un-weight and raise the rear wheel. An un-weighted rear wheel can be steered with the knees and feet and this may be a useful technique on it's own for sharp low speed corners on a descent.

The front wheel lift can be evolved into the wheelie hop whereby a wheelie is used to lift the front wheel over the obstacle. The timing of the wheelie

hop is less critical and is the preferred move for the more advanced rider.

The technique can have sideways or lateral movement added to it to lift the front wheel out of ditches, in this situation more emphasis is required to lift the rear wheel out of the ditch and stop it tracking down the rut and so dragging you sideways down the hill.

The Drop-Off

From the standing neutral position ride off a small drop or kerb, moving your body and thus weight behind the seat then forward again on landing. Practise at low speeds to start with. As you gain confidence and speed, add an upward pull to the bars as you cross the lip of the drop-off allowing both wheels to land simultaneously. On soft muddy landings add more bar lift so that the rear wheel lands first and the bike doesn't stall.

MBL

Bunny Hop

The bunny hop move can be learned and evolved from the two wheel bounce whereby the rider bounces on the pedals, compressing the wheels and tyres and bouncing the bike off the ground. It is this compression and subsequent un-weighting that is the foundation which most on the trail moves are based on.

The two major components of the move are:

      1. coiling the body while compressing both wheels
      2. unloading the compressed tyres and springing upwards

Start off by jumping lines or pieces of tape on the ground before moving onto something higher. An easily dislodged high jump type system using a bamboo cane etc. is better for practice than an unforgiving log or boulder.

Out on the trail this technique is used for subtle un-weighting over small obstacles, to jumping drainage ditches, logs, rocks and other larger obstacles.

Cyclo-Cross Dismount

MBL

At some point you may need to get off the bike. This can be achieved by coming to a stop and putting a foot down, then stepping off the bike, or on the move by doing a "cyclo-cross dismount". The cyclo-cross dismount can be practised at a slow walking speed. **It should be noted that this technique does not work if you dismount above your maximum running speed !**

With both hands on the handlebars and brakes the speed of the bike is reduced to dismount speed. The right leg is swung over the rear wheel and as it touches the ground the left foot is unclipped and a walking or running mode assumed. Once walking or running, the right hand can be removed from the handlebars and used to lift the bike onto the shoulder, using the saddle or top tube whichever is more convenient. The obstacle can then be stepped over or negotiated as appropriate. Practice can make this into a smooth action that is part of the bike rider's range of techniques.

WAYS TO IMPROVE YOUR OFF-ROAD SKILLS

Practice, practice and more practice! However, there are various additional aids which may help you learn or master a technique.

Riding with others who can demonstrate good technique is a great way to "look and learn". However, unless they are willing to be patient and encourage you, they may not make the best riding partners.

Some mountain bike centres have "skills loops" with man-made sections specifically designed to require the execution of more advanced moves. Some may even run skills sessions.

Joining a club which offers regular mountain bike activities can be a good way to improve both riding skills and fitness, as stronger and more skilful riders in a group can motivate others to improve. You can find details of Scottish cycling clubs, some of which are dedicated to mountain biking and many of which have an active mountain bike component, on the Scottish Cycling website (www.scottishcycling.com) or in the SC handbook.

Some riders find they can benefit from the advice of an expert to help them think their way through a move. There are various books written by experienced riders, some of which are listed in the **Bibliography**. There are also a number of DVD's available, providing instruction and inspiration.

Finally, there is a growing number of websites offering advice, photos and video clips of mountain bike skills demos such as www.trials-online.com.

RIDING IN A GROUP ON THE ROAD
Often you will have to link your mountain bike trails with sections of road, so an understanding of group riding techniques on the road will make these sections easier, more fun and, most importantly, safer.

Riding in a group formation gives the riders behind the leaders some shelter from the usual head wind and so makes it easier for the following riders. If the lead riders change regularly, then everyone can share the work and so make the group more efficient. You may have seen this technique demonstrated by road racers in big events like the Tour de France where an echelon forms right across the road. Even with just two riders in a line, the rider drafting at the back can save 30% of the energy expended by the rider at the front.

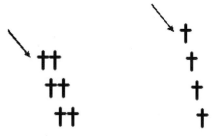

Riders in "echelon" formation
The arrows indicate the direction of the wind

The diagram above illustrates the positions of riders in a formation which gives riders in the group maximum shelter from the wind. If the road is wide enough and traffic is light, riders can pair up to ride two a breast; if the road is narrow or twisty it is safer to ride single file.

Riding in a group requires some practise, good communication and an understanding of what is happening. The group should ride in two lines with the inside line an appropriate distance from the edge of the road. If there are odd numbers in the group, the tail rider can ride in the middle or behind the outside line. Riders should be about 30 cm (12in) behind the rider in front to allow them to benefit from the shelter created.

You should not focus on the wheel in front but look ahead around the rider in front. Stay off the brakes; if you need to reduce your speed momentarily, either stop pedalling or move out and let the wind slow you a bit. If you do have to brake, feather the brakes gently, and be aware of those behind you - warn them of your actions.

The group should have agreed signals and should verbalise or signal movements in advance. This means pointing out potholes, cars parked on the inside, glass etc. Point out hazards and shout, "hole", "rock" etc. The front and rear can advise of traffic, "Car Up", "Car Behind" etc. At predetermined times or distances the leading riders should change. This is accomplished by the outside rider moving across to the front of the inside line, while at the same time the inside line slows down marginally. This is achieved by the inside line soft-pedalling or freewheeling. The overall speed of the group should remain constant. Riders at the rear of the group move to the outside line so completing the chain. The rate of changes can be controlled by the leader by shouting out the changes at set intervals, for example, every minute or kilometre.

The speed should be adjusted to make it comfortable for the weaker riders. A call of "*easy*" from riders feeling the pace, should allow the speed of the group to be adjusted accordingly.

Rules for transitioning also need to be established. To transition from double to single file the inside lead rider slows to allow the outside rider to move in front. This happens all the way down the line from front to back. To move from single to double, the riders scan behind and often the "Clear" command is given from the rear. The lead rider moves to the front outside position, the second rider catches up and the other riders follow moving out and up as appropriate into neat symmetrical pairs.

With practice the above techniques are invaluable for headwind road sections, encouraging a tired group back after a long day's biking and keeping an eye on everyone. Weaker or tired riders can "rest" at the back of the group while the stronger riders work at the front. With good discipline the group shape changes little and allows other road users to be aware of the group and to take appropriate action.

Navigation

By the end of this section Leaders should be able to:-

- Describe the navigational aids available to a mountain biker

- Plan a route using these aids

- Use these aids while on the bike in charge of a group

INTRODUCTION

It is essential that mountain bike leaders, mountain bikers and cyclists who take part in off-road riding and more adventurous touring, acquire an appreciation of the value of good map reading and the ability to use navigational aids and tools such as a compass, route card and bicycle computer to ensure that they are able to undertake journeys by bike efficiently and safely. Don't always leave the navigation to others, and most of all, observe the route that you are following.

Observation is one of the key skills in navigation. In general it should be possible to avoid becoming completely lost by regularly checking your position against the map and route card. By paying attention to distinctive features which you can identify on your map, you can limit the need to use a compass and other navigational aids.

It is worth remembering however, that maps aren't always up to date and some of the information may be missing. Most mountain bike rides involve following a track or trail of some kind which can make navigation easier, but not fool proof. With a suitable map, or better still, a pre-prepared route card, you can monitor your progress against features such as dry stone walls, streams, junctions etc.

It is advisable to make a point of checking your map and/or route card before descending. First check that the map is orientated correctly. Secondly, check whether you have to branch off the track on the way down and how steep, rough or twisty the track is likely to be.

PLANNING A ROUTE

It is good practice to plan your route beforehand. Planning can be done in the comfort of your home or base camp, with the map spread out on the living room floor or kitchen table. Here you can plan where to start and end the ride for day trips, and design a circular route to avoid constant headwinds which can often spoil a good mountain bike day. Your chosen route must be within the abilities of you and/or your group, and it is important to include options for cutting the route short if necessary, and making a quicker return to base.

The mountain biker therefore needs to be familiar with the navigational aids available, be capable of using these tools to plan the route and be able to use these aids while out on the bike.

NAVIGATIONAL TOOLS AND AIDS

The main and essential navigational tools and aids that a mountain biker should be familiar with and comfortable using are: maps, a compass, route cards and a bicycle computer. Two other aids recently introduced and now becoming readily available may be worth considering once you are competent with these basic aids: the altimeter and global positioning system (GPS). Both have now reached an affordable price for many, but they should only be considered if your budget and needs extend to it, and should not be used as a replacement for the basic techniques.

MAPS

Maps have always had a utilitarian purpose and many of the better maps are considered works of art. Experienced bikers are likely to have an extensive collection of well used maps, often preserved with pride and affection, providing memories of past journeys and dreams of future adventures.

Modern maps provide a comprehensive source of very useful information about the areas they cover, presented in a graphical manner. Though extremely useful, they are not always correct, because apart from errors they simply become out of date. In forested areas in particular, new trails are constantly being developed and old trails lost or re-routed as part of forestry operations. In Britain a few organisations have developed a reputation for producing maps of consistent quality and detail to suit the needs of most mountain bikers. The two most commonly used are Ordnance Survey and Harvey.

The sensible cyclist will not venture out on a journey without a map of the area unless that area is very familiar to them. Using a map can add to the pleasure of cycling and provide a wealth of information about the route to be covered.

Planning the proposed route using a map can be a pleasurable experience in itself, and is the most important exercise to guarantee that the route is of a suitable length and has an appropriate degree of difficulty. This is particularly important if some or most of the route is to be off-road.

Which Map and Which Scale?

There are many different map scales. However, the most popular and convenient maps for cycling in Britain are sheets from the Ordnance Survey range using the scale 1:50,000 (O.S. Landranger Series). This means that 1 centimetre on the map is equal to 0.5 kilometres on the ground. Maps of 1:50,000 scale are divided into 2cm 1km squares and the dividing lines are numbered along both sides, plus top and bottom edges of the map using numbers between 1 and 1001 thus forming a grid. Each 100 x 100 km square is allocated a 2-letter reference as part of the National Grid and these letters are clearly marked on each map sheet and used in map reference numbers. Some map sheets contain the boundaries of two 100 km squares and will therefore have two sets of 2-letter references.

The area covered by each 1:50,000 scale map is 40 x 40km, but in many instances adjoining maps overlap to some extent. O.S. sheet maps are numbered beginning with No. 1 (North Shetlands) through to Nos. 203 and 204 which cover South Cornwall. The grid numbering on the edges of the maps goes from West to East along the top and bottom and from North to South down each side.

Though the O.S. Landranger maps are probably best for most cycling and easier mountain biking, the more detailed 1:25,000 O.S. Explorer Series is more appropriate for upland, moorland and remote areas, the greater detail helping with route selection and planning for mountain biking. These maps are also divided into 1km squares. About 300 Explorer maps and up to 50 Outdoor Leisure maps have replaced more than 1200 Pathfinders. Both of these new series are also 1:25,000, but each map covers a greater area than the old Pathfinders. All Outdoor Leisure maps will be in a 30km x 20km double sided format to give extra value for money, and the Explorer maps will come in two formats, 30km x 20km single-sided or 20km x 20km double-sided. The area to be covered will decide the format to ensure that popular local features are fully covered on each map.

Mapping Software
An increasingly popular and valuable tool for route planning, digital maps have the advantage of being seamless, i.e. having no edges, and offering the viewer the chance to see a virtual landscape in 3D. Both Anquet (www.anquet.co.uk) and Memory-map (www.memory-map.co.uk) are based on 1:50,000 and 1:25,000 OS maps and feature a gazetteer, 3D viewing, route planning tools and compatibility with GPS.

Knowing the Legend
Familiarisation with the legend or key of an Ordnance Survey sheet will provide foreknowledge of the types of road or track and other terrain to be covered. Main 'A' roads are coloured red and identified by the smaller classification numbers, with A1 and A11 more major than, say, A123 or A1234. Routes can be planned using mostly tracks and bridleways which are marked with either double or single dotted lines, 'B' roads coloured orange, plus lanes and unclassified roads coloured yellow.

All over the country new roads and trails are being built and existing ones modified, so it is important to purchase maps that are as up-to-date as possible. In the more remote areas fewer changes take place with time and maps several years old may remain adequate.

Map Symbols
Knowledge of the map key where all the symbols are listed is essential. This key however, also needs a degree of interpretation. On 1:50,000 and 1:25,000 maps every solid black line indicates a boundary which is either fenced, walled, or hedged and that is all you know about the indicated boundary. When there is an unfenced boundary to a road or wood then you have a dotted line. Hence you can have a dotted line running parallel to a solid line indicating a track fenced on one side but not the other. Twin

dotted lines indicates an unfenced track. A dotted line sometimes seen around the edge of a forest is not a footpath as many people think, rather it indicates a boundary which is unfenced. On a 1:25,000 map every fence / hedge / wall is marked so you can use the relocation skills outlined below quite easily when in rural areas. There are a couple of exceptions to the rule above; pylon lines, a railway line (both are marked differently on the different scales of map) and high water mark on a coastal area, are all quite distinct from a boundary line.

The map can also indicate hazards, such as a very sharp bend at the bottom of a hill, or a difficult junction with a main road. A leader who takes note of these features is prepared when they get there.

Measuring Distance

Once you know the scale of a map it is a relatively simple matter to measure the length between any two points in centimetres and convert this into distance along the ground; 1cm is equivalent to 500 metres on the 1:50,000 maps and to 250 metres on the 1:25,000 maps. Nearly all compasses are marked with a centimetre scale. The grid lines on Ordnance Survey maps are spaced at 1km apart, irrespective of the scale, so it is possible to estimate distance quite easily by counting the number of grid squares separating the points. It is useful to know that the diagonal from corner to corner of a grid square is approximately 1.5km apart. A map measurer (opisometer), many of which have a choice of scale and are calibrated in kilometres and miles, will enable the approximate length of a journey to be read off, by wheeling the instrument over the intended route on the map, though a check on their accuracy is required. Corrections for slope can be added as indicated later in this section.

Understanding Map References

A map reference number is used to locate a specific place on an Ordnance Survey Map. The full reference number is made up from the following in the order as listed:

1. The two **letter** reference of the particular 100 km square. Note that a single map sheet may contain portions of two 100 km squares

2. The particular **map sheet number** from No. 1 to No. 204

3. The **three numbers** from the map grid on the **bottom** or **top** edges called 'Easting'. For any particular place, read the two digit number from the West side of the one km grid square in which the place lies, estimating the extra tenths towards the East to form a three digit figure

4. The **three numbers** from the map grid on the **side edges** called 'Northing'. For any particular place, read the two digit number from the South edge of the one km grid square in which the place lies, estimating the extra tenths towards the North to form a three digit figure

Using this system it is possible to give any place on any map a location reference. For example, take the Scottish Centre, Dounans at Aberfoyle. The Map Reference is NS 527012. This map reference is made up as follows. The Centre lies inside the 100 km square 'NS'. It is situated between grid lines 52 and 53 reading along the bottom edge of the map, approximately seven tenths towards the East, so the location is given 'Easting 527'. Looking up the left or right hand edge of the map the Centre lies less than quarter way between grid lines 00 and 01 and is therefore given 'Northing 012'. A simple phrase 'along the passage and up the stairs' should help to remind that the **top/bottom numbers are always given before the side numbers**.

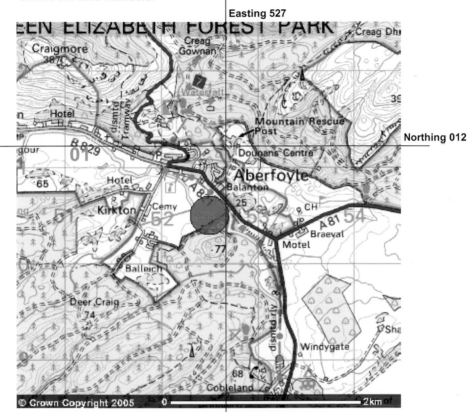

O.S. Grid ref. for Dounans Centre NS 527012

Understanding Relief and Contours

The contour lines on a map are the most important features to the road cyclist and mountain biker. Valley roads often make for a flat, fast route. Hilly routes can be tiring at first, but as cycling fitness develops, climbing hills becomes a challenge that can be enjoyed, and descending is always great fun. Hill tops provide wonderful views on a clear day and roads along a ridge are worth identifying so that the you can stay on high ground longer. Contour lines are a very reliable map feature, even when the ground is covered in snow.

Contour lines on Ordnance Survey maps are brown lines which join points of equal height above sea level. These lines have their respective height indicated at intervals. The 1:50,000 and 1:25,000 O.S. maps show the heights in metres with 10m spacing between contour lines. If the contour lines are close together this indicates a steep slope, whereas widely spread contour lines show the area to be much flatter. By studying the contours the severity of climbing and descending on a planned route can be easily determined. Interpreting the contours on a map involves relating the spacing and shape of the contours to the visible terrain. Some of the common contour features are shown in the map section below.

It takes some practice to interpret contours. It is good to get into the habit of trying to interpret contour features when you are on a ride, even if it's not really necessary for navigation at the time. By matching up ground features with the contours on a map you can build up a repertoire of images in your mind which you will store away for use on future occasions.

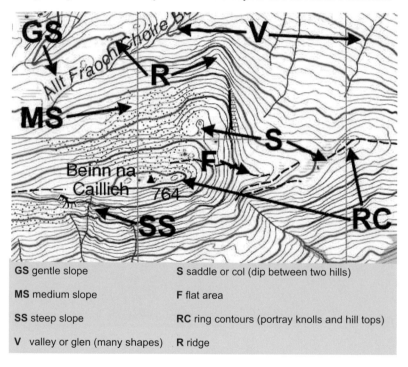

GS gentle slope	**S** saddle or col (dip between two hills)
MS medium slope	**F** flat area
SS steep slope	**RC** ring contours (portray knolls and hill tops)
V valley or glen (many shapes)	**R** ridge

Slope gradients

If a road shows ===>=== this symbol indicates a descent or climb of between 1 in 7 and 1 in 5. The symbol for steeper than 1 in 5 is ===>>=== with the arrowheads always pointing downhill.

Gradients can also be expressed in percentage terms with 1 in 5 being 20%, whereas 1 in 7 is 14% and 1 in 10 is 10%. Modern road signs now use this method of gradient marking. An understanding of this system is useful to the mountain biker.

Off-road gradients can be worked out by counting thick contours within 1cm of the map. The table at the top of the next page shows the relationship between slope angle and the spacing of thick contour lines.

Table showing the relationship between slope angle and the spacing of thick (10m height interval) contour lines on a map.

Slope Angle	Number of thick contour lines in 1cm of map	
	1:50000 map	1:25000 map
10°	2.0	1.0
15°	2.6	1.3
20°	3.5	1.8
25°	4.3	2.2
30°	6.0	3.0
35°	7.0	3.5
40°	8.0	4.0

The distance added by the terrain is not great but once it exceeds a slope angle of 20° it will become significant. The following table explains.

Slope Angle	Additional Distance
10°	1.5%
20°	6%
30°	15%

Off-road slopes of greater than 30° are usually unrideable, at least uphill, and only rideable downhill for those with the required level of skill.

THE COMPASS
The Chinese discovered the principles of the compass some 5000 years ago and these principles remain unchanged today. The compass is little more than a magnet suspended in the earth's magnetic field. It has been and remains the mainstay of the explorer and adventurer and is an essential tool of the mountain biker. Modern compasses are light robust and generally easy to handle in adverse conditions. Specialist compasses are available for most requirements.

A recommended compass is one with a base plate with a romer (measurement scales) on it as well as a magnifying glass. Silva produce a wide range, the Type 4 preferred by hillwalkers would also be suitable for mountain biking. Suunto is another company that makes a similar model usually a little cheaper.

The terminology of the compass needs clarification before describing the skills using a compass you might employ on a ride. The *Base plate* is the oblong plastic plate with scales on it. *Housing* is the circular capsule in the base plate with lines on the bottom, points of the compass and degrees marked around the dial. Inside floats the *needle*. There are various arrows; *Marching* or *Direction of Travel* arrow down the centre of the base plate, *Housing arrow* on the bottom of the housing with additional parallel lines (it points to the N on the housing dial). The *Needle* **is not an arrow,** it is magnetic and floats in the housing. It will always point to the earth's magnetic pole.

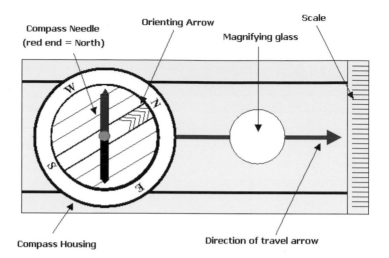

Compass Needle
(red end = North)

Orienting Arrow

Scale

Magnifying glass

Compass Housing

Direction of travel arrow

Warning: your bike might have an affect on the needle if you use it too close to your bike such as resting the map on your handle bars whilst taking a bearing. The compass responds to the earth's magnetic fields but will also respond to other magnetic fields. Any object containing ferrous metal will distort the earth's magnetic field and this can cause erroneous readings on the compass.

THE CYCLE COMPUTER

Most, if not all cycle computers operate by receiving signals from a sensor (mounted on the forks or rear chain stay) that detects the number of wheel revolutions that have taken place. The sensor sends these signals to the computer unit that then turns these signals into useful readings using other information available to the computer such as time etc.

Setting up the computer

In order to get accurate values of speed, distance etc from your computer, you must calibrate the computer properly. To calibrate the computer it is necessary to measure the circumference (L) of the wheel accurately. This is a relatively simple task and gives a more accurate reading than relying on pre-set values (usually supplied in a table in your bike computer's manual). Mark a starting point on the ground, and using the valve as a reference point, roll one full wheel revolution. Mark the ground at the end of the revolution and measure the distance between the two marks. Each cm of wheel revolution is equivalent to approximately 23cm over a 1km (in the range of 207-210). This means that every unit you are out when setting up the computer will give an error of 4.8 metres over 1km.

THE ROUTE CARD

One of the important rules of group leadership is that you must leave details of your intended route with someone who can raise the alarm should you not return before your expected deadline. Whilst this can be seen as the principle reason for producing a route card, there are other extremely useful benefits in so doing. Preparing the route card forces you to consider in some detail the demands which the particular route is going to make on your party. It involves the estimation of distance, time, ascent/descent and compass bearings in the comfort of home or base camp. It also reminds you to consider ways of cutting your journey short should it become necessary.

As an aide memoir it helps you monitor progress; you may never need to refer to the map. If checked against your computer you will be able to work out average speeds should you use this route again. It is probably best to work in kilometres and to have your cycle computer set up in kilometres; this avoids the need for any conversions.

SMBLA

Scottish Cycling, The Velodrome, London Road, Edinburgh, EH7 6AD
Tel 0131 652 0187 E-mail smbla@scottishcycling.com www.scottishcycling.com

Route Card

O.S. Map(s):

Cumulative Distance (km)	Grid ref.	Navigational Feature or Point of Interest	Intermediate Distance (km)
Start			
End			

Escape / Alternative Route(s):

1.

2.

3.

Date:	Start time:	Expected finishing time:
Base / venue:	Group Leader:	Phone / Mobile no.

Additional Comments (transport details, parking facilities, river crossings, viewpoints, food stops, and other useful info)

A full version of the route card on the previous page can be found in the Appendix). A well prepared concise route card can easily be slipped in and out of pockets or clipped to the handlebars for quick reference.

THE ALTIMETER

Atmospheric pressure reduces with altitude at a rate of approximately 10 millibars for every 100 metres of altitude above sea level. So if we measure the atmospheric pressure at any particular point, it should give us a reading for our altitude at that point. Altimeters measure air pressure and are calibrated to read height above sea level. Today they are relatively inexpensive and available in wrist watch or bicycle computer format and cost little more than a good quality compass. It is possible to navigate without an altimeter but there are situations when a knowledge of height may help you pinpoint your position, perhaps in the absence of other features or in situations of poor visibility. The altimeter however has some drawbacks, the main one being its inability to distinguish between pressure changes brought about by altitude and those brought about by changes in weather. It is important therefore to reset the altimeter before the journey starts and throughout the day at places such as spot heights, trig points etc where the height is known. This keeps the altimeter up to date with pressure changes caused by the weather.

GLOBAL POSITIONING SYSTEM (GPS)

Satellite technology has now become affordable to many exponents of outdoor activities. GPS models are becoming cheaper, better and more readily available. GPS uses a number of orbiting satellites each of which transmits a timed signal which is picked up by the receiver on the ground. Signals from several satellites (minimum of 4) are necessary to fix the receiver's position. The greater the number of signals, the greater the accuracy of the fix. Accuracy is now within plus or minus 15m horizontally, but up until quite recently they were only accurate up to plus or minus 100m to prevent their use as guidance for more sinister reasons. GPS should be viewed as an aid to other navigational techniques and not as a replacement for conventional map and compass skills. The need for batteries and the effect of temperature on battery life makes GPS less reliable than conventional methods in extreme situations.

The GPS is possibly best used in mountain biking for re-location or confirmation of your position. This requires switching the machine on to get a fix, then off again once you have confirmed your position. This helps preserve battery life but may minimise your ability to use some of the other features of your GPS.

NAVIGATING OUT ON THE TRAIL

Orientating (Setting) the Map

An important aspect of map reading during a journey is positioning the map so that the visible features correspond with your location and the direction you are facing. This technique is called 'setting the map'. Instead of reading the map as printed, the map sheet must be turned so that real life visible features are aligned with the map. Roads, waterways, farms and hilltops are all ideal major features to assist in setting the map to the same direction as the landscape. Once the map is correctly orientated it becomes much easier to accurately decide on the most appropriate route to take. When riding off-road, setting the map is even more important, but may be more difficult. Without man made features to work with it may be necessary to locate and study closely hill contour lines, valleys, natural high spots, wooded areas, streams and lakes. In good visibility you can set the map by eye. If identifiable features are not visible, for example obscured by mist, you can set the map by using a compass. Use the needle to find north and line up the north on the map with north on the ground.

Monitoring Progress
Using your cycle computer and route card you can monitor progress and in most cases avoid the need to refer to other navigational aids. If you don't have a calibrated computer use the romer on your compass and refer to the map to check the distance you have covered. The romer is a ruler marked on some compasses that allows you to read off the distance between two points. Be sure to use the romer matching the scale of map you are using.

Using The Compass When Unsure Of Your Route Or Location
Much of your map work should be straight forward, simply orientating or setting the map based on the features around you. But what do you do when faced with a choice of tracks in a forest not all of which appear to be marked on your map? First set the map accurately using your compass. Hold the map in one hand and simply drop the compass on your map, rotate the whole map until the compass needle points accurately to the top of your map. It is now set, put the compass away and see if any of the tracks on the map appear to line up with the tracks on the ground.

Map to Ground Bearing
If the above does not convince you a more accurate way is to take a bearing on the map along the track you wish to follow. Place the side of the compass (or a baseplate line) along this track (remembering to have the compass the correct way around). Turn the housing until the N is pointing towards the top of the map and ensure that the housing arrow and lines are aligned with the N/S grid lines (an initial estimate of the bearing in your head will ensure you do not align them with the E/W lines, you can ignore the needle).

Now take the compass off the map and add the magnetic variation, around 5 degrees. Holding the compass in front of your body with the marching arrow pointing away from you Turn your body around until the needle is pointing to the N and check which track on the ground most aligns with the direction the marching arrow is pointing. That should be the track you take, but be vigilant and check the contours, bends in the track and streams you cross until you can verify you have the right one.

Ground to Map Bearing

What should you do when you feel very lost? You will have an idea within a couple of kilometres as to where you might be. Going back to your last known point is one way of relocating yourself. If you have passed some streams, track junctions or the edge of a forest, gone under a pylon line etc. go back to that point and take a bearing along that linear feature. Line up your compass by eye with the marching arrow pointing along the line the feature takes. This must be very accurate; get yourself exactly in line with the feature you are looking along and hold the compass up towards your eye level.

Keep the compass in this position as you turn the housing until the needle points to the N and is resting above the housing arrow. This is the bearing that the feature runs along. Subtract the magnetic variation, put the compass back onto the map with the N pointing to the top of the map and the housing arrow and lines lining up with the N/5 Grid lines in roughly the area of map you think you are (Ignore the needle it will now only tell you if your map is orientated and at this point it is not relevant).

Keeping all the lines lined up, slide the whole compass around on your map until the edge of it aligns with a feature the same as you took a bearing along (a stream or track etc.) Does this have a junction with a track that you might be on? If so that is where you are, orientate your map and try to confirm your location by observing other features around you. If this does not convince you move on and try another feature. When you think you have relocated yourself, you need to confirm this by looking for other features you pass along your route that you should be able to identify on the map and on the ground.

The sequences above are the exact opposite of each other. Both methods can be used in relocation situations. Taking a bearing along a feature on the ground and putting it onto the map is usually less accurate than taking the bearing from the map. If seriously lost, the map to ground system may have to be done a number of times while you work out which stream you might be on. The ground to map system may solve the problem with only one bearing.

Slope Aspect

If utterly lost you may need to do the same as above but using contours only by measuring a slope aspect (the direction it faces). In the same way that you took a bearing along a track for instance, you take one looking down or possibly up a large slope near you. It is important that the marching arrow is pointing directly down the slope as accurately as possible, such that if contour lines were marked on the ground you would be aiming to cross them at 90 degrees.

Once you have your bearing subtract the magnetic variation and place your compass on the map as before with all the lines lining up and the N pointing to the top of the map. Now slide the compass around in the area you think you might be until the compass edge crosses some contours at 90 degrees. You are likely to be somewhere along that line. If there is more than one place that you could be you have to work out a way of eliminating it down to one place. It might be a case of heading along your track for 1 km and if you come to a stream you are in one place if not you are in another, and carry on from there.

Re-section

If you are travelling along a track and wish to get an idea of whether you might have missed a turning or not you can do a re-section. This skill is useful when you are not really lost but need to accurately confirm your location.

First identify an object up to a kilometre or two away, a farm or hill top for instance which you can recognise on the map and the ground, and which is approximately at right angles to the line of your track. Now use the ground to map bearing (re-section). Point the marching arrow at the object, rotate the housing until the needle points to the N, subtract the magnetic variation, place the compass on the map. The edge of the compass (or one of the inner lines) must pass through the centre of the farm on the map, align the base plate so that the housing lines line up with the N/S grid lines with the N towards the top of the map. Where the same edge of the base plate crosses the track is where you are. Double check the plate is still passing through the farm on the map.

You can do this up to three times using different objects but you are unlikely to be more accurate than to within 100m. One re-section is usually sufficient when you are on a linear feature, a second resection might just confirm your position. If you are in the middle of a moor and not on a linear feature marked on the map then several re-sections are required and you need to draw lines on the map down the side of the compass when all the housing and N/S lines are aligned. When you have two lines drawn which cross each other you should be at that cross on your map.

Estimating Time

Estimating distance on a bike is quite simple provided your cycle computer is working and properly set up. Estimating time is somewhat more difficult and speed varies greatly depending on the variety and type of terrain encountered. For rough estimates, double the time you take to cover the same distance on road for forestry roads and farm tracks, and triple the road time for any length of double or single track.

Naismith's Rule

Naismith's rule provides a means of estimating how long it will take to travel from point A to point B. The rule is based on an average walking speed of 5km per hour, with 1 minute added for every 10m height gained. Although Naismith's rule was originally developed for walking, it can be easily modified for mountain biking.

Experience has shown that the average speed over a 3-4 hour ride can be between 8-12 km per hour, although speed varies greatly on different terrain. When climbing, a mountain biker will only be slightly faster than a walker, about 7kph., plus half an hour for every 300m of climbing. On descents 15kph-30kph can be averaged.

Derek Purdy in his book, Advanced Mountain Biking, suggests a modified "Naismith's Rule". The figures used below are for example only; you should establish your own averages for accuracy.

Example:

Route 30km, total out and back, rising 600m.
Outward leg uphill **15km/7kph + (600m/300) x 0.5hr = 3.14 hrs**
Downhill home leg **15km/15kph = 1hr**
Estimated total time: 4.14 hrs or 4 hours 8 minutes.

Few routes would be this straight forward but using experience and this method, accurate timings could be achieved. Reasonably accurate estimations will only be achieved by monitoring your own and group performances on a number of routes.

FURTHER SOURCES OF INFORMATION

The Bibliography lists several reference books on navigation.
A very useful interactive tool to guide you through the principles of navigation with map and compass is "Virtually Hillwalking" which is available to download from the resource library of the **sport**scotland website www.sportscotland.org.uk.

Weather

By the end of this section Leaders should be able to:-

- Explain how weather should be considered in planning a ride
- Understand the factors influencing local weather conditions
- List appropriate sources of weather forecasts
- Interpret weather forecast information and describe some of the visible indicators of weather conditions
- Know the safety implications of extreme weather

 There is a Scottish saying "if you don't like the weather, wait a few minutes". The only certainty about the weather in Scotland, particularly in upland areas, is its instability. Weather systems are constantly passing over the British Isles bringing frequent and sometimes unpredictable changes in weather conditions. The geographical position of Britain makes it subject to several influences on its weather: prevailing south-westerly air flows bringing mild, moisture laden air from across the Atlantic (the so-called Gulf Stream), air flows from continental Europe (generally cold in winter, warm in summer), cold northerly air from the Arctic, and warm southerly air flows. The complexity of influences makes it difficult to forecast both the exact nature and timing of changes in weather patterns. However, local forecasts are usually sufficiently accurate to enable the Leader to make informed decisions when planning and leading a mountain bike ride. Recent weather should also inform decisions on route choice, as factors such as rainfall and temperature will affect ground conditions.

SOURCES OF WEATHER INFORMATION

National weather forecasts on television and radio are most people's source of daily weather information. Although these are usually up to date and therefore reasonably accurate, it should be remembered that national weather forecasts are general forecasts biased towards centres of population and therefore temperatures and wind speeds are given for sea level. Regional TV and radio networks will give more local forecasts, but they are not necessarily detailed enough to predict weather in upland areas. Despite all the technology available to today's meteorologists, predicting the exact timing of weather changes which will result from a developing weather system is difficult. For this reason you should always obtain a forecast as close to your time of departure as possible.

Local bulletins may be posted in tourist information centres, outdoor shops etc. These can be very specific and accurate, and a leader should seek out their whereabouts in advance of a trip.

Telephone/fax weather forecast services are readily available. The fax numbers for the UK Met Office's Weathercall service in Scotland are 09065 300 133 (10-day forecast + 2-5 day regional forecast) and 09060 100 418 (5-day regional forecast). The Weathercall telephone numbers for Scottish regions are listed in the table below.

WEATHERCALL BY PHONE	
Dumfries and Galloway	09014 722 070
Central Scotland and Strathclyde	09014 722 071
Fife, Lothian and Borders	09014 722 072
Tayside	09014 722 073
Grampian and East Highlands	09014 722 074
West Highlands and Islands	09014 722 075
Caithness, Sutherland, Orkneys and Shetland	09014 722 076

To use Weathercall by phone simply dial the number for your area and choose from the list of options:

Press 1 for 10-day regional outlook forecast
Press 2 for the forecast for your town, covering the next six hours
Press 3 for a barometric pressure reading
Press 4 to leave your address to receive a Weathercall Card

Calls cost 60p per minute from a BT landline.

The UK Met Office also provides forecasts for mountain areas. These include information on hazards (blizzards, persistent heavy rain, gales, storms, extensive hill fog, significant wind chill), the height and extent of the lower cloud, and freezing level (the level above which you are likely to find ice on the ground, or where any precipitation will be falling as snow). The mountain forecast numbers are listed below.

NUMBERS TO DIAL		
	MetFAX (£1 per minute)	Premium rate phone (60p per minute)
Index page for Mountain products	09060 100 400	-
MetFAX helpline (telephone)	-	08700 750 075*
MetFAX helpline (fax)	08700 750 076*	-
West Highlands	09060 100 405	09068 500 441
East Highlands	09060 100 406	09068 500 442
2- to 5-day forecast chart	09060 100 426	-

*Calls to the MetFAX telephone or fax helplines are charged at the standard price plan rate from your mobile, or at the national rate from your home phone in the UK.

The Internet is possibly the best source of weather information with many sites dedicated to mountain areas. A good starting point is the Met Office's website – www.meto.gov.uk from which you can access MetWEB, online weather data, including weather reports for outdoor activities. There is a charge to set up a MetWEB account, thereafter forecast information is either free or pay-as-you-go. Find out the best websites for your intended area in advance. On the hills a (web-enabled) WAP phone can be used to access some of these websites.

Local radio stations provide updated forecasts at frequent intervals, and some give forecasts for outdoor activities (hill walking, sailing etc). A small radio will allow access to local weather reports when on the move.

INTERPRETING WEATHER AND WEATHER FORECASTS

A basic understanding of some of the features of weather charts will help to make interpretation of weather forecasts easier. The lines seen on a weather map are called isobars and they plot areas of equal air pressure. The spacing of isobars gives an idea of the strength of the wind; tightly packed isobars represent strong winds, widely spaced isobars mean calm conditions. The wind direction is more or less parallel to the isobars.

The two basic types of weather systems which determine our weather in the British Isles are Low pressure (depression) and High pressure (anticyclone). High pressure occurs when the weather is dominated by stable conditions. Because of these stable conditions, cloud formation is inhibited, so the weather is usually settled with only small amounts of cloud cover. As isobars are normally widely spaced around an anticyclone, winds are often quite light. High pressure systems can be identified on weather charts as areas of widely spaced isobars, where pressure is higher than surrounding areas.

In winter the clear, settled conditions and light winds associated with high pressure can lead to frost and fog. The clear skies allow heat to be lost from the surface of the earth by radiation, allowing temperatures to fall steadily overnight, leading to air or ground frosts. Light winds along with falling temperatures can encourage fog to form; this can linger well into the following morning and be slow to clear. If high pressure becomes established over Northern Europe during winter this can bring a spell of cold easterly winds to the UK. In summer the clear settled conditions associated with high pressure can bring long sunny days and warm temperatures. The weather is normally dry, although occasionally, very hot temperatures can trigger thunderstorms.

A low pressure system occurs when the weather is dominated by unstable conditions. The weather is often cloudy and wet. Isobars are normally closely spaced around a depression leading to strong winds. Low pressure systems can be identified on weather charts as an area of closely spaced isobars, often in a roughly circular shape, where pressure is lower than surrounding areas.

MAKING YOUR OWN OBSERVATIONS

Looking at the clouds can help us to predict the weather. High wispy clouds, known as cirrus, indicate changing weather, and an approaching warm front. Cirrus clouds can develop into thin, milky cirrostratus clouds which can produce a ring of light round the sun or moon, a good sign of rain arriving later. Small, white detached puffs of cotton wool type clouds, known as cumulus, indicate stable conditions or light showers. However, if they expand upwards to form towering masses of dark cumulonimbus cloud, this is a sure sign of heavy showers of rain, snow or hail, sometimes accompanied by thunder and lightning. Learning to "read" the sky is a valuable and fun way to make use of the visible clues around us. The Met Office's website has some useful pages on understanding and observing the weather, including cloud formations (www.meto.gov.uk/education/cirriculum/lesson_plans).

LOCAL INFLUENCES ON WEATHER CONDITIONS

The weather experienced in any specific location is a product of the prevailing weather conditions and the effect of various local influences, most important of which are altitude, aspect and exposure. These factors can have the effect of making the prevailing weather either more or less severe. In contrast to the unpredictable nature of the prevailing weather, the effects of altitude, aspect and exposure are more predictable and even follow some easily remembered rules. The leader should have an awareness of these effects and how they should be taken into account when planning a route and preparing for a ride.

Altitude

Air temperature decreases with increasing altitude at the rate of approximately 1°C for every 100 m climbed. This relationship between altitude and temperature is known as the Lapse Rate. In addition to this decrease in temperature, there is an acceleration of winds on high ground.

At 600m the wind speed can be three times what it is a sea level. The combination of these two effects leads to a much greater wind chill factor. The other effect of altitude is related to the drop in atmospheric pressure as height is gained above sea level which makes it more likely to be cloudy and wet. Low cloud reduces visibility and makes navigation considerably more difficult.

Aspect
The effect of aspect on weather is largely concerned with the timing and amount of sunshine a slope receives. A south-facing slope will always be warmer than a north-facing slope which receives less sunshine. As a result, moisture evaporates more quickly from a south-facing slope and both air and ground temperatures will be higher. In months with snowfall and freezing temperatures, snow will lie longer and the ground will remain frozen for longer periods on north-facing slopes. The other effect of aspect is felt daily as the sun rises in the east and warms an east facing slope early in the day, then as the sun moves overhead, west-facing slopes receive more sunshine later in the day. This daily pattern is felt more acutely in winter when there are fewer hours of sunshine and what little sun there is has a bigger impact on local air temperatures. Camping on a southeast facing slope is the best choice if you want to wake up to early morning sunshine.

Relief / Exposure
Independent of altitude and aspect, the degree of exposure of a slope or open ground will determine how much shelter there is from winds and rain, and from strong sunshine. The exposure factor is effective on a small scale (e.g. leeward side of a single tree) and on a large scale, manifest as "rain shadow". An area in rain shadow receives "shelter" from prevailing rain-carrying winds by a mass of high ground forcing the air to rise and cool, thus causing it to deposit its moisture load as rain. As the air descends to the lee side of such a mountain range it warms and dries, so little or no rain falls. An area such as the eastern Highlands receives much less rainfall as it benefits from this rain shadow effect.

Relief can also alter the strength and direction of prevailing winds. Wind can be funnelled through a valley, becoming much stronger than expected, as well as coming from unexpected directions.

EFFECTS OF SINGLE WEATHER ELEMENTS ON THE GROUP

Wind
Wind is the element which has the greatest effect on cycling, both on and off-road. A cooling breeze in summer can be welcome, but a strong gusty wind can be both annoying and dangerous. The strength of the wind will have a big impact on the effort required to cycle and the speed of travel. In general, allow

more time to complete a route on windy days, especially if crossing exposed ground where there is little shelter. It may be harder keeping a group together as the wind will take a greater toll on smaller or weaker riders. A strong wind also makes communication within the group more difficult, especially when trying to shout upwind, so a degree of team work is required, and frequent checks to make sure all riders stay together. How to ride as a group on the road is explained in the Core Skills section.

The other effect of the wind on mountain biking, especially side winds, is to make the bike harder to control . The best strategy on a very windy day is to stay low, shorten a route or find alternatives with more shelter from trees, and if possible head out into the wind and return with a tail wind which is better for safety and group morale. You can take advantage of shelter provided by trees, hedges and leeward slopes on the windward leg of a journey.

Anyone venturing out on a cold windy day has experienced the effects of wind chill. A stiff cold wind will whip heat away from a warm body much faster than if the air were still. If clothing or exposed skin is wet, this heat loss will happen even faster. Carrying appropriate wind-proof clothing to reduce wind chill is essential (see Clothing section).

Rain

On a short, easy ride on good tracks light rain is not a problem if the group is prepared to get wet. Keeping on the move should prevent anyone from getting cold. On a more challenging ride even light rain can add to the technical difficulty, affecting ground conditions and visibility. Smooth surfaces like slabs and tree roots can become especially slippery. In wet conditions choose a route which keeps to well surfaced tracks and forest roads; not only will this make the going easier, it will minimise damage to soils and vegetation. Persistent rain can take the pleasure out of a day's ride and a good leader should assess group morale with this in mind. Wet weather riding also takes its toll on bikes, wearing brake blocks faster and requiring chains and moving parts to be cleaned and lubricated thoroughly after a day's ride.

Snow

Riding in the snow can be a fun experience but is does present its own challenges to route finding and bike handling. Falling snow restricts visibility and can cut off routes very quickly. **Note: a Mountain Bike Leader can only lead a group in winter conditions with the addition of the relevant on-foot qualification (i.e. Mountain Leader Winter).** Under the terms of the Adventure Activities Licensing Authority (see Legal Issues & Liability) permissable conditions for a Leader with an MBL award only are "some snow (e.g. a light dusting) or avoidable patches, or lightly freezing conditions (e.g. an overnight frost) prevalent or forecast.

Sun

Strong sunshine is the perfect antidote to cold, wind and rain, but it does carry its own risks, even in Scotland. Cyclists are more prone to sunburn than walkers as the breeze created while riding has a cooling effect and burning of unprotected skin can go unnoticed.

Mist

The obvious effect of mist or low cloud is to reduce visibility, increasing the level of concentration required while riding and the need to navigate accurately.

EFFECTS OF EXTREME WEATHER CONDITIONS

Hypothermia

Hypothermia, or "cold exhaustion" is usually brought about by a combination of factors, of which wind chill is highly significant. Coupled with physical exhaustion, being excessively cold and wet can lead to a lowering of the body's core temperature and a disruption of normal bodily functions and behaviour. How to deal with hypothermia is covered in Emergency Procedures, but it should be noted that cases require hospital treatment, so prevention is far better than cure. Hypothermia can be avoided by use of appropriate clothing, especially wind proof garments in very cold winds, and waterproofs to prevent getting soaked and losing body heat through evaporation. Keep energy and fluid levels up to prevent fatigue and boost the body's ability to deal with the cold. On very cold windy days, a leader should seek as much shelter for the group as possible and limit the duration of exposure.

Heat exhaustion

The combined effects of strong sun, physical exertion and dehydration can lead to heat exhaustion, and eventually sun stroke. Leaders should be aware of the potential for this to occur and be able to recognise the common symptoms – acute headache, nausea and fatigue. Drinking copiously in hot weather is vital to prevent heat exhaustion developing, and exposed skin should be protected from strong sun.

Lightning

The chances of being struck by lightning are relatively small, but the risks are greater when outdoors and can be reduced by taking appropriate action when a storm approaches. The safest place to be is within the area of a conductor which will conduct the lightning to the ground. This could be a mast or tall post which is standing alone. Under a tree or an overhang is a bad place to shelter because the lightning will try to bridge the gap to the ground by the shortest route, which will be through you if you are sitting underneath. You can, however, seek shelter within a wood or group of trees. Although being in a car is a safe place to be, being on a bike is not. If you are caught out in the open the best strategy is to crouch down with your hands on your knees. Do not lie flat on the ground. Stay away from natural lightning rods such as camping equipment, and from rivers, lakes, or other bodies of water.

Emergency Procedures

By the end of this section Leaders should be able to:-

- Understand how the interaction between external factors and the group characteristics determines the level of hazard

- Explain how planning can play a part in preventing emergencies

- Know why it is important to have a strategy for managing an emergency

- Describe how, as a group leader, you would implement an emergency strategy

- List what equipment to carry to be prepared for an emergency

INTRODUCTION

An 'emergency' might be a delay due to minor repairs, a damaged unrideable bike, an injured immobile person or quite likely a combination of several of these. It does not just affect the group, but also those waiting at base. It will involve sound leadership, communication, and planning. If these have been applied before leaving base, then hopefully your emergency procedures are a case of *prevention being better than a cure.*

Most organisations will operate to written guidelines in accordance with the Adventure Activity Licensing Authority (AALA). This section will add support to those guidelines. 'Late Back' procedures are particularly relevant to mountain biking. There is also guidance on emergency procedures and equipment to be carried.

It is difficult to consider emergency procedures without considering the general management of an outing. Before looking at emergency procedures we should briefly consider the range and type of likely problems and hazards.

HAZARDS

Mountain Hazards can be classified into three main groups: weather, terrain and people. They are usually all interlinked and it is the leadership or lack of it that determines the effects of any combination of hazards. The mountain bike leader has the additional element of mechanical equipment to contend with.

Weather affects our comfort and environment continuously. Terrain challenges our equipment, skills and experience. People relates to leadership, experience and judgement, with respect to the group, equipment, weather and terrain. The first two only become hazards when we venture out into them unprepared, inexperienced and unskilled.

Cycling at night is another issue and should only be planned for experienced riders with proper effective lighting systems. Dealing with emergencies at night as opposed to in daylight is a much bigger challenge. Neither TCL or MBL awards equip a leader for planned group night riding, only for emergency procedures which may involve, by necessity, riding outwith daylight hours.

Good supervision is not being in the right place to witness the accident, it is being in the right place to ensure it never happens. The majority of accidents concern judgement and leadership decisions. Often these are made before leaving base. The mountain bike leader, with the added equipment factor must weigh up a lot of issues, especially when a group meets with some individuals producing their own bike for the first time. Is the bike suitable for the proposed journey? If not what am I going to do about it? Reaching a solution may lead to a difficult confrontation with a parent, but you have safety, the rest of the group, your boss, your employer or organisation and other parents to consider. **Who are you responsible to?** or **Who is your client?** are big questions.

If a bike is not suitable for an intended journey, failures of a mechanical nature could lead to serious injury. Whilst a mechanical failure leading to a sudden incident might on the face of it be due to a bump in the track or insufficient bike skills, one might ask was it a reasonably foreseeable accident if the quality of the bike is considered in relation to its rider, the nature of the route selected and possibly the prevailing weather conditions which will affect the terrain? Could a decision to walk a section as opposed to riding it make a difference? If that is the case should you lead by example and walk it also?

Ultimately much of this is linked to experience which in turn leads to judgement. Many problems are resolved by firm decision making, based on a weather forecast, previous knowledge of the group and your chosen route. Having alternative route options up your sleeve gives a further safety net for making up time or avoiding more difficult terrain. Set a cut off time by which you should start a given route and have an alternative planned should you not meet the deadline. Mark these on your Route Card (see Navigation section). You can inform your base of your change before leaving or phone on the way to the start point.

Your subconscious, sensible / common sense thoughts need to become conscious thoughts on which you can express an opinion and act.

STRATEGIES FOR MANAGING AN EMERGENCY

Mobile phones, whilst extremely useful for all sorts of reasons do not provide a reliable strategy for dealing with emergencies. You may not be able to get a signal in remote areas. Even if you do manage to phone for help it may be some time before help can get to you.

How do you manage the incident as a whole from the second it happens to the point when you finally crawl into your bed at the end of the day? Don't forget that looking after the casualty is only half of the problem, looking after the rest of the group can be a major part of managing an emergency. There are three basic steps which will dictate the outcome of the incident. They may well happen very quickly but missing one of them could compound the situation considerably.

ASSESS THE SITUATION AND MAKE A PLAN

1. Prevention of any further incident
Instantly assess the situation, ensure your own safety, the safety of the rest of the group and then ensure no further harm can come to those who are injured. For example, if somebody has a crash, do not slam on your brakes and risk crashing yourself or bringing other riders down. Do not run headlong towards the casualty and risk tripping and injuring yourself. Avoiding panic and staying calm can prevent a second accident occurring all too easily.

If riding in failing light these are very serious issues. Ensure that no one else could crash into the scene. Put people behind and ahead to warn other users of the hazard and try to get the casualty and equipment off the track into a safe area, not onto the outside of a bend for example where others might be likely to overshoot.

2. Administer any repairs or first aid
It may be useful to delegate a number of minor tasks to other members of the group to keep them occupied and together. Go up or down the track to warn other users of the hazard, check over the other bikes for any damage, make the casualty comfortable, collect water from a nearby stream etc.

3. Planning for evacuation
All too often a couple of people are sent for help and then the leader realises that they could move the injured party to a more suitable location either for shelter or for ease of access for the emergency services. Not only have those you sent for help then got the wrong grid reference, they are not there to help you move the equipment or injured person either. Taking time to make your plan will, in the long run, save vital time.

Every emergency is different and there is no set solution. At an incident you usually have three main options to consider before working out a plan:

1. Self help is always preferred providing no further harm will be done
2. Send for help
3. Call for assistance and wait for someone to find you

Calling for assistance to come is a serious step to take. The standard call for help in the hills is six shouts, whistle blasts or torch flashes, then wait a minute and repeat. The reply is three shouts, whistles or torch flashes. If no one is around, your rescue may depend on you having left a Route Card with a responsible person who will raise the alarm, based on the organisation's 'late back' procedures. Alternatively, on well-populated tracks someone may come by who can help, they may have a mobile phone or be able to go quickly for help leaving your group intact to look after the injured person. Beware being bounced by their enthusiasm to assist and letting them rush off for help before you have made a plan. This may also lose your control of information dissemination to unwanted parties, the press etc. Your base contact / employer really needs to hear the facts of the situation from you first, not through a parent or, in the worst case scenario the press.

Sending someone for help needs careful thought. Control of information is vital. You will probably need to control access to a phone. With a group of minors there should always be a second adult in the group and available to assist. Either they or you should go for help alone or with one other reliable person. Beware of sending a large group of youngsters just to get them out of the way; they can slow your rescue plan down and once a phone is available may become difficult to control. In addition; should the emergency services wish to be guided by those you have sent for help they will probably only be able to manage one or two passengers. You will then be faced with splitting the group further which creates other problems of in 'loco parentis' and information control / containment.

Self help could include support from your base. It should be stressed that this is only possible when no further harm is likely to be done. A major issue that is often overlooked is the amount of additional equipment each person finds themselves carrying once an injured person is being supported. It is not just their equipment that has to be passed around but also the equipment of those doing the supporting. Equipment can be left for a while and shuttled along with a casualty or returned to once a safe location has been reached. Self help can bring out the best in people, often having a bonding effect on the group.

In reality a combination of the above strategies is often used with the group making their way with a casualty down the route that the emergency services will approach from.

A MESSAGE FOR HELP

What should go in a message for help? The sample accident report form in The Appendix can be used to record the information which you will need to relay to the emergency services. The sheet can be photocopied and kept in your First Aid pack with a pencil. Carrying it with you is easy and saves you, in what is already a very stressful situation, having to think about what to try and record. You can also delegate the writing to someone else in order to involve the group and keep them busy. Sound navigation skills become essential in order to provide an accurate grid reference. A six figure grid is accurate to 100m which is adequate. Additional information is always helpful e.g. "where the track enters the forest".

Help with damaged equipment or minor injury may be sought from base. **Help with a casualty requiring evacuation or hospital should be sought through the police (dialling 999), who have statute responsibility for any accident and co-ordinate rescues.** They may call for Mountain Rescue assistance if ambulance access is difficult. Do not rule out helicopter rescue for which you may need to get the casualty to an open area. Ensure you give people the number of the phone you are using and remain by it until the police pick you up.

Finally, once the casualty is picked up you will be faced with another decision; to go with the casualty to the hospital or to stay with the group? If things are working well and you have good procedures at base, hopefully relatives/friends of the casualty will have been informed and can get to or be taken to the hospital. People at base should sort this out. It may be that your assistant could go to the hospital with the casualty, in which case they may need to be prepared for meeting parents. You may have to meet the rest of the waiting parents in order to go through what has happened. There is also the rest of the group to consider; they may need the opportunity to talk with you once they have recovered back at base.

It is advisable to try to record on paper what happens as a serious incident runs. Though this is difficult you should find time to take a step back and jot a few thoughts. Often delegating minor tasks to the rest of the group keeps them usefully occupied and gives you some breathing space.

EMERGENCY EQUIPMENT

What do we carry and what can we do with it?

A **bike repair kit** needs to be adequate (see **Trailside Repairs** section), including tools to service the range of bikes in the group. Various improvised repairs can be made with duct tape, spare cables and some zip ties.

What/how much equipment to take should be balanced with what can sensibly be repaired when out on a wet cold day. For dealing with emergencies other than mechanical failure the following items should be spread amongst the group:

First aid kit

Include surgical gloves, large wound dressings, bandages and triangular bandages. These are particularly useful for the common injuries which result from unexpectedly parting company with your bike.

Group shelter

To accommodate all the group. A survival bag or a space blanket are not really recommended. A group shelter such as a Bothy Bag, available in various sizes accommodating from 2 to 12 people, should be sufficient.

Whistle, Map, Compass, Pencil and Paper

Think about how you would insulate a casualty from the ground on a wet muddy day. Using the group's rucksacks leaves a problem of what to do with their contents and what the rest of the group might sit on in the wet inside a group shelter. A foam sleeping mat can be cut into sections and carried wrapped around cross bars or lining rucksacks which makes them easily available to sit on. Sections of the mat can also be used for splinting. A large piece of bubble wrap (cheap and very light to carry) is great for insulation and warmth when someone is lying on the ground.

Food and Drink

A small thermos of hot liquid or a stove and pan with a brew kit can do wonders for morale and warmth under a group shelter.

Other items

Spare clothing - hats and gloves, waterproofs; torches, mobile phone or money; clean water for cleaning gravel rash.

Improvised Stretchers

Improvising a stretcher is only an option when no further harm is likely to be done to the casualty. It can also become a very time consuming affair. In general their use should be limited to moving the casualty to a place that is safer or more sheltered or provides easy access for the emergency services.

Whatever is quick and simple is the best solution, often using a group shelter or survival bag. It appears as a decisive action and requires little explanation. One can envisage constructing a stretcher across two bikes using foam sleeping mat and poles of wood lashed across them, or making a stretcher to be dragged along the ground behind a bike. This all takes too long, requires more equipment, energy and skills and carries the risk of causing further injury. It is likely to be safer, quicker and more practical to walk, carrying or supporting the casualty, than to support and push them on a bike, especially up or down hill.

Summary

Planning and preparation should reduce your chances of being faced with an emergency

Remember your clients are not just those you are leading

Being properly equipped should help you to deal with an emergency

Make a plan - no two incidents are ever the same - try to stand back and take time to plan effectively

Control the spread of information

Bike Set-up, The Safe Cycle & Trailside Repairs

By the end of this section all Leaders should be able to:-

- Explain why correct bike set-up is important for cycling

- Describe the principles underpinning basic riding positions

- List the basic tools required for trailside repairs and explain what repairs they can be used to effect

- Fix a puncture and a broken chain, and know how to adjust gears and brakes

- Demonstrate knowledge of more advanced repairs and their limitations, given the equipment available and remote terrain **MBL**

- Effect advanced hillside repairs to enable a bike to be ridden back to base, considering additional expedition equipment being carried, such as panniers **Expedition**

INTRODUCTION
Cycling on or off-road is a marriage between rider and machine. How happy this marriage is depends to a large extent on a good fit between bike and rider, and on having a bike in good working order. Learning how to set-up a bike and repair it when things go wrong are essential skills for any cyclist, and these need to be well developed by any leader in charge of a group off-road.

BIKE SET-UP
If a cyclist is to function optimally on a bike then the bike must be made to fit the cyclist and not the other way around. The Leader should be aware that a general riding position should fulfil three basic requirements:

1. Safety – so the cyclist can control the bike at all times, especially the brakes

2. Comfort – to enable the cyclist to perform for a given duration through a variety of terrain and conditions

3. Efficiency – for optimum power output at any give time

In seeking a good position, many cyclists have used trial and error but few have the sensitivity to judge whether they have achieved their optimum position. They adapt to a position rather than the position being adapted to them. Young and novice cyclists are those who most need advice - a short session under expert guidance can improve efficiency, safety and comfort.

The **saddle position** should be established first, with the handlebar position then being determined in relation to the saddle position for the particular type of mountain biking. The handlebar position must be safe with easy access to the brake levers.

After cyclists have found their correct position, they should be encouraged to record their individual position measurements to make it easy to replicate their position on a new or borrowed bike. With children however, it should be noted that these measurements can change dramatically during periods of rapid growth.

Despite the advice which follows, it is important for the Leader to take into account how a cyclist *feels* on a bike. With the infinite variations in the human body, no single method can precisely predict bike positions. Saddle height preference depends on the type of cyclist, their anatomical geometry, the chosen type of mountain biking and stage of development.

Basic Riding Position

For introductory or general mountain biking, the saddle height is perhaps the most important adjustment to the bike with regard to *fit* and position on the bike. The height is measured from the centre of the pedal axle up the seat tube to the top of the saddle. Optimal saddle height is a compromise between efficiency, aerodynamics, safety and comfort.

A simple approach to finding a good saddle height starting point is to sit the cyclist on their bike with their heels on the pedals. Set one pedal to its lowest point (in line with the seat-tube) - the leg should be straight, without being stretched. There should be no rocking of the hips as the cyclist

pedals backwards. With the balls of their feet on the pedals (correct foot position), the knee will be slightly bent when the pedal is at the bottom of the pedal stroke. Pedalling with the ball of the foot over the spindle of the pedal gives a more efficient and comfortable position.

If this position is found to be too low it may be necessary to raise the saddle 1-2 cm above this point. If the saddle is raised there should be no rocking at the hips, when observing the pedalling action from behind. Novice riders learning to ride a bike may require a lower saddle position that allows them to easily put both their feet on the ground.

Handlebar Position

Handlebar position must be safe, allowing easy access to the brake levers. It is important that the reach to the brakes is checked as children and female riders will need a shorter reach.

In pool or hire bikes there may be limited opportunities to alter this position. The handlebar position can be altered by changing the stem height and/or length. Length adjustment will require replacing the stem, however, most bikes now use "A-head" stems which can be easily removed. Placing spacers above or below the stem neck decreases or increases the height respectively. Such stems can also be flipped 180 degrees and mounted "upside down" so changing the effective stem angle and height. Bear in mind that any alteration of the stem angle or height will also affect the reach as the head-tube of the frame in which the forks sit (and on which the stems clamps) is at an angle (commonly of 73-74 degrees). For mountain biking the emphasis should be on comfort and safety, the rider does not want to be overstretched or too cramped on their bike.

Measurement Card

Once cyclists have found their optimum position, it is useful to record all the important adjustment positions so that the position can be duplicated as and when required. The following measurements should be recorded:

Saddle height - (along the line of the seat-tube centre of pedal axle - top of the saddle)

Saddle setback – (distance, measured with a plumbline, from the nose of the saddle forward/backward to the bottom bracket axle centre)

Difference between saddle height and top of handlebar height (easily done using a spirit level and ruler)

Reach - (centre of the saddle - centre of the handlebars)

Remember that during growth phases in young riders these measurements can change quickly.

Sample Measurement Card	
Set-up feature	**Measurement**
Saddle height	
Saddle offset	
Difference between saddle height and top of handlebars	
Reach (saddle to handlebars)	

The information provided above gives the basic guidelines on establishing bike position. As the type of riding or the rider specialises in a particular mountain bike style or discipline the position may change from the basic start position. For more downhill or technical styles of riding a lower saddle height is preferred, whereas longer distance cross-country riding usually results in some fine tuning of the basic position for comfort and efficiency.

TRAILSIDE REPAIRS

All leaders should be able to effect most common repairs to enable a bike to be ridden back to base, such as puncture repair, mending a broken chain and adjusting gears or brakes. The more remote the environment or technical the terrain, the higher the level of mechanical ability required, and the more comprehensive the toolkit and spares list will have to be.

Bike Checks

Bikes should be checked thoroughly before setting out so that any obvious mechanical problems can be avoided, and also to ensure that there is a suitable range of tools to fix all bikes in the group. Appendix E contains a **Bike Safety Checklist** which you can use to systematically check every bike before use and record any repairs or adjustments which need to be made. This routine check should be part of a *generic risk assessment* for every planned outing (see **Hazards & Risk Management**).

Tools for the job

Having the right tools for the job is essential to making a quick and efficient repair. As well as checking bikes before you set out, check the condition of your tools and clean them after use. Using a dirt-encrusted tool is a sure way to wear out the bolts on your bike as the grit acts like sandpaper between the tool and bolt. Metal tools will rust and soon become useless, so keep them dry between rides.

Just as bike component technology has advanced in recent years, so has the development of bike-specific tools. Hence, it is generally better to source your tools from a bike shop rather than from a DIY store to make sure you get the right tools for the job. There is now a great choice of multi-tools available which combine several tools in one compact unit.

A word of warning about multi-tools: functionally can be compromised by compactness and the desire for lighter weight. If you opt to carry a multi-tool then check that it performs as expected before relying on it to carry out a repair on a ride.

For example, some multi-tool chain tools do not open up enough to insert a Shimano joining pin, and so are useless for fixing a broken chain.

Always opt for functionality over light weight and aesthetics when it comes to choosing your tools. Sometimes it is worth opting for a sturdier "workshop" model of a tool such as a chain splitter which makes light work of splitting a chain, especially with cold hands when you have a waiting group to manage. Longer Allen keys give you more leverage, and those with "ball" rather than square heads make it much easier to access bolts from awkward angles. A bike mechanic, rather than a front-shop sales assistant, is probably the best person to advise you on tool selection with respect to their functionality and suitability for the job.

TOOL CHECK LISTS
The lists of tools and spares below are divided up into basic kit, to be carried by all Leaders, and additional kit which MBL and Expedition Leaders should carry. The lists are by no means definitive. The **Expedition Planning** section contains more information on expedition kit.

BASIC TOOLS AND SPARES KIT

Tools
Pump (should adapt to fit Presta and Schraeder valve types)
Tyre levers
Allen keys (2, 2.5, 3, 4, 5, 6, 8, 10mm)
Torx key T25 (to tighten disc bolts)
14mm socket (for crank bolts)
Chain tool (make sure it will fit a Shimano joining pin)
Crosshead screwdriver
15mm pedal spanner
Spanners (if required for brakes or to remove wheels)
Shockpump (plus adaptors)

Spares
Inner tube(s) (a Presta valve fits any rim)
Puncture repair kit (check it is complete and glue has not set)
Tyre patches
Lube
Cable ties
Duck tape
Spare brake and gear cables
Spare chain link and joining pins (for SRAM and Shimano chains)

Additional tool kit for Mountain Bike Leaders
Tools
Spoke wrenches
Pliers with cable cutter (a multi-tool such as a Leatherman will have other useful tools too)
Crank remover

Spares
1/2" coach bolt
4" long 9/16 bolt and nuts (emergency pedal)
Spare seat pin bolts (specific to bikes being used)
Spare gear hangers (specific to bikes being used)
Spare (folding) tyre
Superglue

Expedition kit

Hypercracker or similar tool for removing cassette
A selection of spare nuts, bolts and washers
Pannier and trailer spares
Swiss army knife
Each individual should carry brake blocks to fit their bike, and spare spokes (or multi-fit Kevlar spokes)

Repairs
As a group leader you must not only be familiar with your own bike, but also be able to confidently make repairs to any bike in the group. It is a good idea to have a training session to demonstrate basic repairs to a group, especially where experience is lacking, and to cover any variations in components of the bikes belonging to each group member (obviously, the latter is not an issue with a fleet of identical bikes provided by an outdoor centre). Involving each group member in a repair job is a good way to encourage team work and will make repairs on the trial quicker and more fun.

It is beyond the scope of this manual to provide a comprehensive guide to carrying out bike repairs. There are many bike repair and maintenance books available which can make even more advanced repairs seem easy (some are listed in the Bibliography). Working on your own bike will teach you a lot about the best way to do repairs and the importance of a bit of prior planning and organisation! You may decide to further your knowledge by attending a bike maintenance course which some colleges, clubs and bike shops run.

The following websites may also be of use:
Maintenance courses www.edinburghbicycle.com
Maintenance tips www.webmountainbike.com

Clothing

By the end of this section Leaders should be able to:-

- Appreciate the advantages of cycle specific clothing

- Understand the layering system

- Suggest various ways to control body temperature during a ride

- Recommend clothing suitable for a variety of riding conditions

DESIGNED FOR THE JOB

To many people cyclists' clothing may seem strange; it is usually close-fitting to stop garments flapping in the wind or catching on the bike, and made of high-tech stretchy fabrics. You don't have to be an experienced cyclist to appreciate the advantages of cycle-specific clothing. Kitting yourself out with even just the basic items can improve your protection from the elements, your comfort and your ability to move around on the bike. A good bike shop, and many outdoor shops, should not only have a range of cycle clothing for you to choose from, but will be able to advise you about the type of clothing suited to your riding and the time of year.

CYCLING SHORTS

If there is one piece of clothing that will really improve your enjoyment of cycling, it is a good pair of cycling shorts. Worn next to the skin, they have a padded insert and flat, well placed seams to greatly improve comfort whilst riding. They come in a variety of fabrics, but those made of a wicking material offer the most comfort and all round use, as shorts in summer and under cycling tights or longs as it gets cooler. Recently, baggy shorts with a padded liner, removable or attached, have become popular as they provide a more socially acceptable look than tight lycra! Women's shorts are also available having a padded insert and cut designed to suit the female anatomy.

HELMETS

Your head is the most vulnerable part of your body when cycling and should always be protected. In some countries it is compulsory. A helmet is especially necessary when you are riding in rocky unknown terrain, though you never know when you might crash.

The main things to check when buying a helmet are that it fits properly and meets the safety standards set and tested by institutes such as Snell or ANSI (in the US), EU (Europe), BSI (Britain) or AS (Australia). This will be marked inside the helmet. In order to be effective in a crash a helmet should fit your head like a glove. You should be able to feel the helmet on the top of your head and it should move with your scalp when you wiggle your eyebrows. It should fit low on your forehead without obstructing your vision to the front or side.

 The more you spend on a helmet the better ventilated it will be and the fit system will probably be more adjustable and more secure too, resulting in increased comfort and better protection should you crash. **Helmets should be replaced regularly (at least every five years) whether they have had an impact or not as the polystyrene degrades through time, use and contact with UV rays.**

In the example above the dial on the back allows infinite adjustment to give a comfortable and secure fit. The position of the straps can be altered using the locks below the ears.

EYEWEAR
Whilst it is vital to protect your head from a potential crash, it is just as important to protect your eyes from the glare of the sun, flying insects, spray, grit and other debris that can be thrown up from the trail. The sudden impact of an object hitting your eye while riding can be enough to momentarily blind you and make you lose control. Of course you can spend a lot of money on a pair of shades if you want to make a fashion statement, but you can purchase as a set a frame and choice of lenses for different light conditions quite cheaply.

FOOTWEAR
Cycling shoes with drillings for attaching cleats which clip into pedals are recommended. They come in a variety of styles to suit your riding. Cleats offer safety and efficiency advantages; being attached to the pedals by a "ski-binding" type quick-release keeps your feet on the pedals when spinning fast or riding over bumpy terrain. Having a firm attachment to the

pedals also allows a better pedaling style to develop, and is more efficient. The soles of cycling shoes are very stiff to reduce foot fatigue and give more efficient power transfer. Racing shoes will have an almost rigid sole, but there are more flexible shoes available which are a bit more comfortable should it be necessary to walk any distance in them. Finally, cycling shoes tend to have Velcro closures rather than laces, which if not tucked in can get caught in your drivetrain and cause a nasty accident.

Overshoes, made of neoprene or wind/waterproof fabrics, add the final touch of insulation for your feet during the winter months, when toes can get very cold on the bike due to the wind-chill factor.

GLOVES

Gloves are also recommended, enhancing the grip on the handlebars when the hands get hot and sweaty, and in the rain. They protect hands from brushing against trees etc and from gravel rashes during a fall. They vary from (fingerless) track mitts to full winter gloves and are available with or without padding. These days, with suspension forks being almost standard on mountain bikes, the padding function of gloves is not as important as grip.

DRESSING FOR THE WEATHER

In a day's off-road riding you may experience wind, rain, sun and extreme temperature changes as you change altitude and ride through sheltered and then exposed areas. There are many "technical" fabrics and garments, that are designed specially for these varying conditions.

During a ride many adjustments will be necessary to clothing to maintain an optimum working temperature. There is a tendency to heat up on the climbs and cool down greatly on the descents. Temperature control is achieved through the use of zips, windproof, breathable and wickable technical clothing, and making use of the layering system.

THE LAYERING SYSTEM

The layering system is the term given to a flexible and practical clothing system which allows you to adjust for changes in both the weather and your activity level. The system comprises of layers of clothing which can be put on or taken off depending on the conditions. There are three basic layers in this system and they are:

1. Base Layer

This layer is next to your skin and can make a big difference to your comfort. The base layer should be made from a fabric which transports (wicks) moisture away from your skin and helps to keep you dry and comfortable during and after activity. The best fabrics for the job are made from synthetic yarns which have been engineered for maximum performance and are of the type found in sports/thermal underwear.

2. Mid Layers

The mid layer function is to provide insulation from the elements. The most popular modern mid layers are constructed from fleece fabric which are available in different weights. Fleece is not only extremely warm for its weight, but also allows moisture from the wearer to pass through it readily.

3. Shell Layer

The shell or outer layer is the barrier to both the wind and rain. The most effective shell garments are constructed from waterproof and breathable fabrics with taped seams, which not only keep the rain out, but also allow vapour to escape. The price of a shell garment increases exponentially with the breathability of the fabric and the number of features (as each seam/zip has to be taped). Only vapour can pass through the fabric, not moisture, so the more breathable and well ventilated your jacket is, the less likely you are to suffer from condensation collecting inside it – it's worth spending the extra if you can afford it.

Access Rights & Responsibilities

By the end of this section Leaders should:

- Understand the principal features of current access legislation in Scotland, England and Wales

- Be aware of your responsibilities as a Leader when accessing the countryside

- Be familiar with the Code of Conduct for Off-Road Cycling

- Know where to look and who you might contact for more information on access, rights of way and off-road routes

INTRODUCTION

Mountain bikers, and especially leaders of mountain bike groups, must demonstrate consideration for the environment and for others living and working in or using the outdoors for a wide variety of pursuits. Public perceptions of mountain biking as an activity which has a damaging impact on the environment and poses a safety hazard to other users may be largely unjustified, but they highlight the need for mountain bikers to demonstrate responsible behaviour in order to cultivate mutual respect with other land users and the general public, and to show that mountain biking can be conducted with courtesy and sensitivity at all times. This is particularly important as the countryside comes under increasing recreational pressure and its users need to be sympathetic to various environmental issues and those whose livelihoods depend on the land.

There has been a strong tradition of recreational access to the outdoors in Scotland which has depended largely on the goodwill of land owners and the respectful conduct of walkers and others enjoying the countryside. This voluntary approach has had mixed success, and in some cases has led to a conflict of interest between different parties or even to criminal action.

This section seeks to explain the current access legislation in Britain, provides some guidelines on acting responsibly in accessing the countryside, and gives various sources of further information on access, rights of way and route-finding.

ACCESS AND THE LAW IN SCOTLAND

Recent legislation, known as the **Land Reform (Scotland) Act 2003**, has established statutory rights of access to most land and inland water for non-motorised outdoor recreation. These new rights, which are conditional on users behaving responsibly, came into effect on **9th February 2005**. Under section 10 of the Act, the **Scottish Outdoor Access Code** ("the Code") was drawn up and consulted upon by Scottish Natural Heritage, with the final version being approved by resolution of the Scottish Parliament on 1st July 2004. The Code provides detailed guidance on the responsibilities of those exercising access rights and of those managing land and water. The document is available from a website managed by Scottish Natural Heritage, www.outdooraccess-scotland.com.

The Code is underpinned by three key principles:

SCOTTISH
OUTDOOR ACCESS CODE

- **Take responsibility for your own actions**
- **Respect the interests of other people**
- **Care for the environment**

Some of the key information contained in the Code relating to off-road cycling is summarised in this section.

Everyone has access rights established by the Land Reform (Scotland) Act 2003 provided these rights are exercised responsibly. You have rights of access to be on and to cross over land and inland water for recreational, educational and certain relevant commercial activities. Access rights include off-road cycling, whether undertaken by individuals or groups or as a commercial activity, where that activity could be done by any member of the public exercising access rights. A Trail Cycle or Mountain Bike Leader leading groups on identifiable tracks and trails as a commercial venture would be an example of this.

Access rights apply everywhere as long as they are exercised responsibly, but certain specified areas are excluded. The main exceptions include: houses and gardens, the curtilage of non-domestic buildings, compounds, building sites, demolition and engineering works, quarries and surface mineral workings, sports and recreational fields *while in use*, fields in which crops have been sown or are growing (but access around the field margins is allowed), schools and school grounds, places which charge for entry, and golf courses (except to cross them, although you should never cross greens or tees). Byelaws, management rules or other regulations introduced by local authorities or other public bodies may prohibit or restrict access.

RIGHTS OF WAY

Public rights of way have been recognised in Scots law for centuries. A route established as a right of way under common law must connect two public places, follow a more or less defined route and have been used by the public for at least 20 years. Many rights of way exist for walkers; comparatively few have been established for cyclists. Cycling is now considered a separate category of use, and as such, a route used by cyclists for 20 years could establish the right to use this route for cycling. Most rights of way in Scotland are not marked on Ordnance Survey maps or signposted, nor is there a legally recognised record of rights of way. The best record at national level is the **National Catalogue of Rights of Way** (CROW) which has been compiled by the Scottish Rights of Way and Access Society (Scotways), in partnership with SNH and local authorities.

The latter hold copies of their local CROW record. All recognised public rights of way continue to exist under the Land Reform (Scotland) Act 2003. Where a public right of way passes over land excluded from statutory access rights, such as through a farmyard or field of crops, the route can still be used as a right of way.

CORE PATH NETWORKS

Each Local Authority in Scotland is compiling a **Core Path List** of paths/tracks/trails of shared use. Currently Core Paths may not be ideally suited for mountain biking, but an opportunity exists for mountain bikers to influence such developments. Mountain bikers are encouraged to seek representation on their Local Access Forum which will provide an opportunity to advocate certain design standards of Core Paths for cycling and help address any access issues.

ACCESS LAW IN ENGLAND AND WALES

A different approach to access has been taken in England and Wales. The **Countryside and Rights of Way Act 2000** (CROW Act), which came into force in England and Wales in May 2005, gives a new right of public access to "open country" and registered common land. The right includes activities such as walking, running and climbing, *but does not extend to cycling*, horse riding or driving a vehicle. However, the new Act does improve public rights of way legislation, and recognises a new category of right of way called a "restricted byway" with rights for cyclists and horse riders. The new access rights are being introduced in England and Wales on a regional basis with a consultation-led mapping of "open country" in each region. The Countryside Agency and the Countryside Council for Wales have produced a new Countryside Code to guide responsible use and management of countryside access – see www.countrysideaccess.gov.uk. The full CROW document can be obtained from: www.hmso.gov.uk/acts/acts2000/20000037.htm.

The current categories of routes which cyclists *can* access in England and Wales are:

Bridleways – an extensive network of tracks open to cyclists and horse riders, blue waymarked

Byways – open to all traffic, usually unsurfaced tracks, red waymarked. Contact the Byways and Bridleways Trust www.bbtrust.org.uk (Tel. 0191 236 4086)

Restricted byways – replaced "roads used as public paths" (RUPPs)

Towpaths – a British Waterways cycling permit is required by cyclists www.britishwaterways.co.uk (Tel. 01923 226 422)

Cycle paths – designated routes (signed for cyclists)

The National Cycle Network – mapped by Sustrans (see "Finding a Route" below)

Cycle tracks – designated under the Cycle Tracks Act 1984

EXERCISING ACCESS RIGHTS RESPONSIBLY

As a leader, you have a duty of care for yourself and your group to ensure that the outdoor environment is accessed responsibly and safely. Remember that as a group you will have a greater impact than a solo rider and you should plan your trip and act accordingly. Doing a site-specific **risk assessment** is recommended for every outing. Speak to the land managers who are responsible for the areas your group intends to use and obtain the permission of the relevant persons if you wish to use a facility provided for other activities e.g. an outdoor centre or school.

In Scotland a **Code of Conduct for Off-road Cycling** was produced in 1995 by Scottish Cycling with reference to recommendations given by the Cyclists' Touring Club (CTC), SNH, Forestry Commission, **sport**scotland and IMBA-UK (International Mountain Bicycling Association-UK). SMBLA will be involved in updating the code in 2005 to fit within the context of new access legislation and the Scottish Outdoor Access Code. A summary of the present guidance from Scottish Cycling is as follows:

Ride with care and consideration for others

Give way to walkers and horse riders on narrow paths, dismounting where necessary. Warn others of your approach and reduce your speed so as not to cause alarm.

Keep to permitted routes

Observe the local access rights and byelaws. Plan ahead to ensure your group is safe and welcome in the areas you are riding.

Respect land management activities

Follow precautions provided for your own safety. Stay clear of farm animals and activities such as tree felling, crop spraying and game shooting.

Maintain access points

Use gates, stiles or other access points to cross walls and fences. Leave all gates as you find them. When you park your bike or a car make sure you are not blocking access for other users.

Care for the environment

Avoid damaging soil, crops and natural vegetation by keeping to paths or tracks and field margins. Follow local information aimed at safeguarding protected plants, animals or geological features.

Help prevent erosion in sensitive areas

Avoid wet, boggy or soft ground or areas where riding churns up the surface. Go through puddles, not round them. Avoid fierce braking on downhill sections and do not skid. Take account of recent weather and the time of year, as these will affect ground conditions.

HILLPHONES

Hillphones is a Scottish telephone answer-machine service which provides information on where stag stalking is taking place. The information is primarily aimed at walkers and climbers, but may also be useful to mountain bikers accessing the hills to plan routes avoiding stalking operations. The scheme originated in the Access Forum and is organised by SNH, the Mountaineering Council of Scotland and participating estates. In 2004 there were 17 areas where Hillphones operated, but these areas are by no means the full extent of deer stalking activity in Scotland.

The Hillphones service runs from 1st August to 31st October each year, covering the height of the stag stalking season. If you are planning to lead a group in the hills, you can call the Hillphone to check the location of stalking activities and which routes within the area are unlikely to be affected over the next few days. Stalking may take place any day of the week but is not permitted on a Sunday.

For a list of the Hillphone numbers and maps of the areas covered go to www.hillphones.info. It may be helpful to have a map beside you when you call the Hillphone.

WHERE TO GET MORE INFORMATION

i. Scotland

Information and advice on access rights and responsibilities, and on who to contact in your local authority is available at www.outdooraccess-scotland.com. You can also contact your local SNH office. The SNH e-mail address for access issues is recreationandaccess@snh.gov.uk.

Local Access Forums (LAFs) have been set up by all local authorities to provide an opportunity for liaison between the public, local authorities and other bodies on any issues concerning the exercise of access rights, rights of way and the development of core path planning. More information about Local Access Forums can be found at www.outdooraccess-scotland.com or from your local authority.

The Paths for All website found at www.pathsforall.org/uk/index.shtml may also be helpful for those interested in paths close to where people live.

ii. England and Wales

The Government Department for Environment Food and Rural Affairs (DEFRA) provides very accessible information on countryside legislation and explains how the Countryside and Rights of Way Act 2000 is being implemented: www.defra.gov.uk/wildlife-countryside/issues/index.htm.

The Countryside Agency is engaged in producing maps of all registered common land and open country in England. Their website www.openaccess.gov.uk shows regional maps in the "provisional" and "conclusive" stages of access mapping, with land designations relating to the Countryside and Rights of Way Act. Equivalent information for Wales is provided by the Countryside Council for Wales: www.ccw.gov.uk.

Access land will be shown on the above websites and on Ordnance Survey maps and tourist guides. O.S. are redesigning their Explorer map series to show access land (in yellow) and increased detail on paths and access routes.

Terrain & Route Selection

By the end of this section Leaders should be able to:-

- Appreciate the main types of terrain for mountain biking and their advantages and disadvantages

- Have an awareness of the current trail grading systems in use

- State clearly the terrain criteria for their level of award – TCL or MBL

- Explain how to make informed decisions about what type of terrain is suitable for a group

INTRODUCTION

The choice of terrain for mountain biking in Scotland, and many parts of the UK is very wide. Some classification of the main types of terrain, and of the current trail grading systems in use may be helpful to the leader in considering appropriate terrain to lead groups in.

BASIC TERRAIN TYPES

1. Forestry tracks

Forest plantations, the majority under Forestry Commission management, offer an extensive network of tracks throughout most areas of the UK. The Forestry Commission's website (www.forestry.gov.uk/cycling) has a searchable database of venues; this includes 103 separate destinations in Scotland alone. Forest or woodland of any type offers shelter from the elements and is usually rideable in almost any weather. Facilities such as car parks and picnic areas are often provided and can make a good place to rendezvous. There are usually a variety of tracks, from forest roads to narrow singletrack, offering a choice of routes of varying difficulty and length. Bear in mind that forest operations may restrict access to some trails, and that unless otherwise signed, trails will be shared with other users.

2. Open hill country / moorland

In contrast to the forest environment, open hill country or moorland offers advantages of better views and visible navigation features in good weather, but because of the greater exposure, this type of terrain can be unpleasant or even dangerous in poor weather. Navigation and visibility may be difficult if foggy or misty, and the lack of shelter from wind and rain can compromise enjoyment and safety. Tracks will vary from established paths to narrow sheeptracks, the latter sometimes appearing to be a good route choice, but often frustratingly petering out or disappearing under heather. Leaders should be aware of access legislation, and respect advisory access restrictions for lambing, deer stalking etc. For more information on checking access restrictions during deer stalking see the **Access Rights & Responsibilities** section.

3. Shared / cycle-specific tracks / paths

This category covers all recognised routes accessible by bike, from canal tow paths, bridle ways, cycle paths and shared footpaths to minor roads. These routes offer easier riding conditions, with better surfaces, shallower gradients and wider tracks. However, other users must be respected and it may be better to seek quieter times or other areas for group riding. Each local authority in Scotland is compiling a **Core Paths List**, a network of routes which can be used for cycling, walking and other activities. Information on the quality of the riding surface, width, gradient etc of these Core Paths is not always available, but all should be rideable on a mountain bike, although perhaps not suitable for road bikes. For more information on Core Paths see the **Access** section.

4. Purpose-built cycle facilities

These include bmx parks, "closed road" circuits and skills loops which may be part of an outdoor centre or sports ground. These are ideal training venues for practicing core skills and offer a leader the chance to assess the abilities of group members. Check whether such facilities have to be booked in advance and what the conditions of use are.

TRAIL GRADING SYSTEMS

There are currently several trail grading systems in place, commonly using symbols and colour coding to indicate the difficulty of a trail. CTC, Forestry Commission and IMBA-UK all essentially use the same system, which grades trails as green, blue, red and black, progressing from "easy" to "severe". The descriptions for each grading category can be viewed at the websites of these respective organisations:

www.forestry.gov.uk
www.ctc.org.uk
www.imba-uk.com

However, the relative standards of a grading system may vary from area to area, or depending on the system used. Current signage may not always make the distinction between trails graded for cycling or those for walking clear, so the red cycling trail may be confused with the "red walking route", for example.

The Forestry Commission, in partnership with SMBLA, **sport**scotland, Scottish Natural Heritage, Cycling Scotland, Visit Scotland, International Mountain Bike Association UK and other countryside organisations, is working towards defining a national off-road trail grading standard which will bring consistency to trail grading throughout the UK. This standard will be applied to existing trails, and used to inform on trail building and trail management in Forestry Commission forests and other sites. It will provide mountain bikers, and particularly leaders of groups, with pre-defined information about routes which is consistent across all sites where the system is adopted.

Trail grading criteria are likely to include factors such as trail width, trail surface, average and maximum gradient, natural obstacles, technical trail features, length of trail and remoteness, as well as some indication of the level of skill and fitness required for each trail category. Improved interpretation and signage will make it easy to follow a trail and provide clear distinctions between designated cycle trails and paths marked for walking.

It is important to note, however, that trails are not graded with a view to leading a group down them, and leaders should follow the advice below when deciding on suitability of graded trails for their group.

GENERAL ADVICE ON TERRAIN SUITABILITY FOR GROUPS
Leaders will need to assess their group before taking them on a trail. The ability of the group decides the terrain, not the ability of the leader, however, both TCLs and MBLs must be fully aware of the terrain criteria which *limit* their scope of operation (see the next page). Remember, these are limits which must not be exceeded, rather than conditions which have to be met for every ride, so a Mountain Bike Leader, after assessing his or her group, might decide to take them on only green ("easy") trails.

SMBLA TERRAIN AWARD CRITERIA

Trail Cycle Leader

Public highways, way-marked routes, rights-of-way on which cycles are permitted, identifiable routes, tracks and trails with obvious navigational features and with low to medium technical difficulty. Routes will be 90-95% rideable and take the group no more than 30 minutes walk by a reasonably fit person away from a shelter with communication, and to be no more than 600 metres in height.

Mountain Bike Leader

Public highways, way marked tracks, rights of way, identifiable routes and tracks with obvious navigational features. Routes can be of high technical difficulty but will be rideable along the majority of their length. The route may be at any height above sea level and may be more than 30 minutes walk from help.

A Trail Cycle Leader could act as an assistant to a Mountain Bike Leader in MBL terrain, and would be encouraged to do so to gain experience of more technical terrain with a view to attaining the next level of award.

TCL and MBL awards are valid in "normal summer conditions" only. The awards and are *not* valid in winter when the ground or weather conditions would require the skills of a Winter Mountain Leader holder to cope, or where such conditions are forecast.

The decision to take a group into any type of terrain, and onto a particular trail must remain with the leader. There are many factors to consider: technical abilities, fitness levels, aspirations, time of year and expected weather conditions, and equipment of each group as a whole.

A Rider-defined Trail Definition model

Whereas a trail-grading system based on pre-defined physical criteria can be applied to man-made trails, and may be helpful to the leader in judging the difficulty of a trail in a particular site, what information can a leader use to assess trails in other areas where there is no such grading in place ?

The model on the page opposite is based on rider-defined criteria and has proven to be a useful tool in assessing trail difficulty in any type of terrain. This model can be used in a number of ways as all the skills required for mountain biking can be condensed into four basic elements: speed, balance, line-choice and power. It has a built-in feedback loop: if you can control your speed, balance, power and line choice this will increase your confidence; as your confidence grows your control of these elements will also increase.

In practice the model is used to assess trail difficulty by scoring how many of the four elements a rider requires to complete a section of trail. If a rider has to be competent in one or two of the model's elements, this can be categorised as easy-moderate, and should be within the scope of that rider's ability. For example, a wide, smooth descent requires a rider to be able to control their speed and possibly understand or be able to weight shift (control balance), thus only two elements are used.

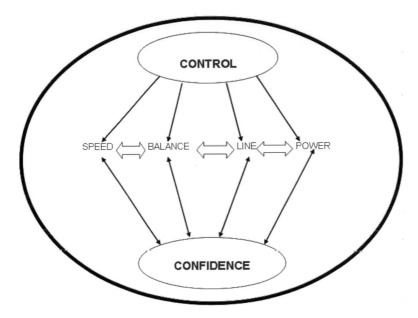

If a rider has to be competent in three or four of the above elements then that trail or section of trail is moderate-difficult and may be outwith the scope of a less experienced rider, but within the scope of a confident and experienced mountain biker. For example, a rolling section of single track littered with rocks and roots would require control of speed, balance, power and line choice.

The model encourages a leader to focus on the ability of the riders in the group when choosing suitable terrain, so echoing the advice given above, the starting point is always the abilities of the group, rather than the nature of the terrain.

As well as helping to match a group's ability to the terrain, the model also allows the leader to modify the degree of difficulty of a trail to meet the group's ability. For example, a twisty descent that requires control of speed, balance and line choice would be moderate-difficult, but if the leader stopped the group and walked them through that section pointing out the line as they went, that would remove the line choice element, so reducing the degree of difficulty of the trail.

Safety and planning
As well as requiring background knowledge of the group, terrain selection and route choice must employ the process of **risk assessment** (see **Hazards and Risk Management**). This may involve a specific risk assessment, pre-riding any routes you intend using to identify and record potential hazards, and controlling any risks to your group. If you are taking the group onto new terrain, the minimum requirements are for a generic risk assessment, along with an ongoing dynamic risk assessment. As part of the planning process you should select one or more alternative routes, as well as short cuts which can be taken if you have to change your plans due to bad weather, group performance, lack of time or an emergency.

It goes without saying that as a leader you must always ride within your abilities to be able to manage a group off-road; you must have physical and mental energy in reserve to be able to move around the group, make decisions and maintain control of any situations which may arise. If the terrain is too challenging for you as the leader, your ability to lead effectively will be severely compromised. If a group's aim is to challenge their off-road skills on a particular trail, ask yourself honestly are your own skills and fitness levels suited to this group's aim?

TERRAIN KNOWLEDGE

There are many practical ways to build up your knowledge of terrain and routes which will help you choose what is suitable for the groups you may be leading. You can develop your own database with notes describing terrain type, variation, route length, access points, shelters, riding surface in different weather conditions etc.

Some suggestions for developing terrain knowledge include:

- Personal riding experience
- Riding with a mountain bike club or group of experienced riders
- Assisting other leaders on group rides
- Accessing first hand information on particular routes, e.g. bike shops, bike cafes, mountain bike centres
- Trail literature, e.g. guidebooks, leaflets, maps
- Recording your own experiences, photographs and annotated maps
- Website information
- Complimentary outdoor activities, e.g. hill walking, orienteering

WHAT MAKES A GOOD TRAIL ?

Though often emotive and very subjective, this is a topic that the Leader should reflect upon. Understanding the basics of good trail design will help the Leader make informed choices to suit the needs of their groups and act as an advocate for better trail design and management.

The International Mountain Bicycling Association provide the best advice on good practice, providing design guidance booklets and information on their websites at www.imba.com and www.imba-uk.com.

Sustainability is perhaps the most important principle for good trails. A sustainable trail will have the following properties:

- Supports current and future use with minimal impact to the area's natural systems
- Produces negligible soil loss and allows vegetation to inhabit the area
- Recognises that pruning or removal of certain plants may be necessary for maintenance
- Does not adversely affect native wildlife
- Requires little re-routing and minimal long term maintenance

Water management is the principle problem for many trails in the UK and the principle cause of erosion when allowed to channel or flow down the trail. Trails sited on the side of a slope, which drain well, are better than muddy trails at the bottom of the slope where all the water has collected.

Contour trails which gently traverse the hill or slope, with a surface that slopes slightly towards the low side, characterise a trail that stays dry and good to ride. Subtle undulations in a trail create grade reversals and grade dips that also defend against water damage by preventing it from tracking down the trail; they are also fun to ride.

Trail systems with loops are appealing because they can offer the most variety. They can offer more technically difficult trails, varying distances and different points of interest. The core of a trail system should comprise trails that are wide and smooth and appeal to a variety of users, the more difficult and technically demanding trails can branch off of the main system. A core trail which is the entrance to the system gets most use; other loops branch from it and become narrower and more challenging. Trails can vary from open and flowing to tight and technical. Good trails have a certain flow and rhythm where one turn blends into the next and every descent leads to another rise. Transitions between the different types of trail are important, to avoid cyclists having to brake hard and skid, causing additional trail maintenance problems.

Natural or established routes are likely to have evolved socially and established as rights of way, or may be estate roads and access routes for management purposes. It is unlikely that they will always follow the principles of good trail design, however many of them rely on volunteer support in maintaining or improving these routes. The principles of good trail design applied to such routes is likely to improve their sustainability and usability. Make sure you get landowner permission before undertaking any "trail improvements".

FINDING A ROUTE

There are many sources of information on finding suitable routes to ride off-road, for example guidebooks, websites and maps. Investing some time researching a good route when planning a trip is likely to be rewarded. See **Useful Contacts** for *Places to Ride* contact information. Cycle route information is becoming available at an increasing rate as the sport of mountain-biking grows and more and more people wish to access the countryside by bike. Some local councils now have cycle-route information on their websites and tourist information centres usually have leaflets and guidebooks covering parts of Scotland. A good starting point is Scotland's National Tourism Board's website www.visitscotland.com.

The **Cycling Scotland** website has a route-finder with a full description of each route, route-gradings, recommended maps and a list of features such as accommodation and cafés along the route: www.cyclingscotland.com.

The **Forestry Commission** actively encourages cycling in their forests, although forestry operations may restrict access to some routes at certain times. Their website contains descriptions of access points and routes for cycling in the majority of their sites across Scotland and the rest of Britain: www.forestry.gov.uk.

The **National Cycle Network** developed by Sustrans, links towns and cities across the UK using minor roads, cycle paths and other traffic-free routes. Some of these are ideal for leading groups of less experienced riders in non-challenging terrain. Sustrans' website contains maps and information on these routes, www.sustrans.org.uk, or Tel. 0117 929 0888.

The **CTC** (Cyclists' Touring Club) holds a large UK-wide database on cycle routes which can be accessed (by CTC members) on-line at www.ctc.org.uk or by contacting them to request route information sheets (tel. 0870 873 0060 / cycling@ctc.org.uk).

Maps are essential to route planning and can offer alternatives if a planned route can not be followed on the ground. Britain's national mapping agency, Ordnance Survey, has maps covering the whole of Britain at the most popular 1:50,000 scale or at the smaller scale of 1:25,000 offering more detailed coverage. A limited number of OS maps can be obtained through the online get-a-map facility, www.get-a-map.co.uk. Cycle tracks are not presently marked on OS map, but this may become standard on 1:25,000 OS maps for paths which are on the **Core Paths List** (once this has been compiled by each Local Authority).

Mapping software is becoming an increasingly popular and valuable tool for route planning. Digital maps have the advantage of being seamless, i.e. having no edges, and offering the viewer the chance to see a virtual landscape in 3D. Anquet (www.anquet.co.uk), Memory-map (www.memory-map.co.uk) and Tracklogs (www.tracklogs.co.uk) digital mapping software are based on 1:50,000 and 1:25,000 OS maps and include such features as a gazetteer, 3D viewing, route planning tools and compatibility with GPS (Global Positioning System) navigation. Digital mapping products allow updated information on real-life and "virtual" features such as access changes to be available to users more rapidly than printed maps for which reprints take longer to appear.

Expedition Planning

By the end of this section you should be able to:

- List the key responsibilities of the expedition leader

- Know the distinction between personal and group equipment, and be able to give examples of both

- Describe different ways of carrying equipment on an expedition, and the relative advantages of each

- Describe the different methods of shelter available

- Outline the range of camping equipment required for an expedition and how to use it

- Understand basic camp craft, including hygiene good practice, and be aware of your environmental responsibilities

EXPEDITION: *A journey or voyage with definite purpose*
Whatever the purpose, a journey over more than one day by mountain bike is likely to require participants to pull together their cycling and other outdoor skills, allied to their knowledge, understanding and appreciation of the outdoors. In this context, it is assumed that mountain bike expeditions will be undertaken by groups of comparatively inexperienced cyclists, led by very experienced leaders.

The great mountaineer and sailor, the late Bill Haman once commented, 'If an expedition cannot be planned on the back of an envelope, it is too big'. However, before undertaking a mountain bike expedition, a group leader needs to ask many questions and make many decisions, even if the final plan is in fact succinct enough to fit on the back of an envelope!

THE PARTICIPANTS
"Who is going to take part in the journey?" is the first, and probably the most important question to be asked by the leader(s) of any expedition. Also to be decided is the size of the group and the personnel who are to be involved in assisting in leading the party during the journey. As a general rule, smaller groups experience fewer problems en route and make less impact on the environment than larger groups.

THE PURPOSE
It is vital that the purpose of the journey is agreed by all and that everyone feels that they wish to commit themselves to its achievement. The more that all members of the group are involved in planning and preparation from the earliest stages, the more likely they are to be fully committed if circumstances become testing.

THE ROUTE

The route must be designed with considerable care so that it enables all members to achieve their aims without being excessively demanding for anyone. Previous experience by the Leader of the intended route or area to be visited is likely to be very valuable. Bearing in mind the time of year, an initial assessment of the possible environmental impact of the group on the area should be made at this stage.

HAZARDS AND RISKS

An assessment must also be made of the hazards which are likely to be found on the route and of the risks that these could pose for members of the group if the right precautions are not taken (see **Hazards & Risk Management**). If some members are not sufficiently able or fit enough as cyclists to attempt the journey, or they lack the necessary expedition skills, it will be necessary to arrange training sessions to help improve their level of fitness and competency. Skills and fitness levels must be matched to the hazards and risks which the route and expected conditions are likely to present.

PERMISSION

In addition to full consent from the members of the group, permission for the venture may also have to be sought from parents or guardians, employers, an education or other authority, land owners, and other countryside users. The leader should check in advance of any route plan whether there might be any land management activities or events which will restrict access to the area they wish to use (see the **Access: Rights & Responsibilities** section).

BIKES AND OTHER EQUIPMENT

If the leader is relying on group members to bring their own bikes it will be necessary for rigorous checks to be made of the safety and efficiency of all machines well in advance of departure. It is also important at an early stage to make an assessment of the likely requirements for continuing maintenance and of the provision of tools and spares during the expedition, as well as the capacity of the bikes for carrying extra load. Depending on the anticipated nature of the journey, it will be necessary to judge what other gear and provisions may be necessary, such as equipment and food for camping, or severe weather clothing. In most cases, members will need to carry more cycle luggage than usual for day-long ventures with, in addition, attention to requirements for extended travel in what might be a remote area.

TRANSPORT

Although the expedition may be wholly self propelled, it is probable that the group will need to make arrangements for travel to and from the expedition area. They may also wish to arrange some sort of vehicle support during the journey.

Carrying Bikes on Cars

What is the best way to transport bikes by car? Whatever method you choose it must be safe, secure and legal. If the bikes are being carried outside the car make sure you remove all attachments (pumps, water bottles, saddle bags, lights etc) which could potentially fall off or become detached during transit. Tighten all straps and fixings fully and double check them just before you leave and at intervals on your journey.

Rear-mounted bike racks, particularly hatch or boot-mounted types, are extremely popular, but when laden with bikes there is usually some obstruction of the car's lights and registration plate. When it is dark this is barely noticeable because the lights shine through the spokes, but there is still a problem with the number plate which must be legally displayed at all times. You can overcome this to some extent by attaching a spare rear plate with rubber bungees. However, to be totally law-abiding and comply with the Road Traffic Act, the Road Vehicles Lighting Regulations and the Road Vehicle (Registration and Licensing) regulations, you need a fully functioning trailer board with all the attendant supplementary vehicle electrics. In the absence of a trailer board you can remove the bike wheels and position the bikes so the gear changer doesn't get in the way. Or, alternatively, resort to using a roof rack.

PLANNING RESPONSIBILITIES OF THE EXPEDITION LEADER

The leader of a mountain bike expedition has to fulfil multiple responsibilities to ensure the success of an expedition. He or she must:

- identify the purpose and aims of the expedition
- complete and record an assessment of the hazards, and risks which the group will face
- have knowledge of current legislation for adventurous activities
- obtain parental consent, clearance from the authority, and relevant personal and medical information
- work out a budget for the trip and ensure that insurance arrangements are made, if necessary
- plan an appropriate route for the group, including escapes to easier trails or roads
- ensure that bikes and other equipment is prepared and maintained in a trail-worthy condition
- obtain and take account of local weather forecasts
- brief the group before the venture and at relevant points during the journey
- arrange and organise transport to the start and from the end point of the journey, if required
- have sufficient experience of extended journeys by mountain bike to ensure he/she is confident all that eventualities can be dealt with
- recognise his/her responsibilities to parents or guardians, individuals of the group and the group as a whole, any sponsoring authority, committee or manager, the general public, local residents and landowners, as well as to other outdoor users and to the environment

PERSONAL AND GROUP EQUIPMENT

Clothing (see also Clothing section)

It is recommended to have two sets of clothing, one set of cycling clothing to ride in and another that is always kept dry to use at the campsite or if the other set gets too wet. This would imply that both sets of clothing can be used for cycling, even if one set is not perhaps cycling specific. It is better to start off in damp clothes and keep the dry stuff dry than to risk ending up with no dry clothes at all. It is important that the leader checks the clothing of the group before setting out that day. Even when using waterproof panniers/rucksacks, sealing clothes and other items that need to be kept dry in plastic bags should be routine. Heavy items should, if possible, be placed at the bottom of panniers, but those items that may be required during the ride or when first reaching a stopping point should be placed on top or in side pockets so they are more accessible.

Carrying kit

There are three main ways of carrying kit, either on your body, on the bike or in a trailer. As the amount of gear carried increases, the ability to successfully negotiate technical terrain decreases. Routes should therefore be planned with this in mind.

Gear carried on the body can either be in a rucksack or bumbag. Carrying much more than can be accommodated in a 25 litre rucksack is going to severely limit your riding ability and will dramatically increase the potential to cause injury either to your back, or to some other part of you when you fall off. It is probably better to carry most of your stuff either on your bike or in a trailer.

Two small panniers firmly attached to a rear rack is possibly the best method. The rack should be strong and secured to the bike at four places by bolts secured by locknuts. A rackpack could be attached to the top of this. A traditional saddlebag is a favoured method of carrying gear by many. If you need to carry more gear than this then front panniers could be considered if the forks allow them to be fitted. Most experienced off road riders have found front "lowrider" style panniers to be too close to the ground, and easy to snag on the narrower trails. Again, the strength and fixing method should be as the rear rack. Some find handlebar bags useful, others find that they obstruct the view of the trail and can interfere with steering. If used, limiting the weight they carry is essential.

Most riders who have used trailers report that a single wheel trailer is the only design worth considering off-road. Tandem riders and those travelling with young or much weaker riders have found them especially useful, as carrying kit for two people on one bike is more difficult. Trailers can be useful for hauling in heavier gear to base camp. However, consideration should be given to the reasons for the trip and the environmental impacts of creating longer term, larger base camps.

Tents

There are many tent designs available, from the more traditional ridge or tunnel design to more modern dome and geodesic designs. Dome, Tunnel and Geodesic tents are very lightweight with the poles being made from very light and flexible fibreglass or, more commonly, aluminium wands (tent poles) which slot through sewn sleeves in the tent itself. The design of these tents maximises the use of floor space due to their steep walls, and makes them easy to move if you decide to change your campsite to another spot in the immediate locality. These tents are also incredibly strong as they are designed to flex with the wind rather than try to stand up to it and eventually buckle.

Ridge tents are classic pieces of camping equipment and still remain popular today. Although heavier and usually bulkier than the other three types of tent, they are incredibly robust and durable which makes these a good choice for group and extended use when the tents may be up in one place for a number of days. Ridge tents can be pitched flysheet first in a storm, so are a better choice for wet weather.

Ideally all tents should be lightweight, waterproof (even under heavy rain), condensation free and fitted with a sewn-in ground sheet and down to the ground fly sheet. Modern single skin breathable tents can be very light, however they are often more fragile, condensation can be more of a problem and they can leak after a season or two. A two layer tent, outer flysheet and inner, is heavier but can be more reliable, as well as often providing more room under the flysheet for cooking and gear. A tent with a covered porch is great for storing grubby panniers, and may also provide a shelter to cook under in bad weather. Tent areas used for cooking should be easily vented to avoid build up of steam and therefore condensation, as well as build up of toxic gases. The entrance to the tent should be large enough to allow you easy access to the inner tent and should be designed so as to keep out driving rain and snow.

Most lightweight tents suitable for mountain bike expeditions will be classified as 1-3 person tents. One-person tents are designed for the solo camper, whilst the 2-person tent is designed for the very comfort-conscious solo camper or a duo. Two-person tents offer the best compromise in terms of weight, space and pack-size. It is probably not worth trying to carry a tent for more than two or three people, as even splitting it between this number, the parts will be quite heavy. Similarly, a 3-season tent is probably the most versatile for UK conditions, being fully waterproof and tougher than a 2-season tent. Only if you expect to be camping in winter conditions or high winds do you need a 4-season tent.

In summer you can get by quite adequately using bivvi bags. This may be a useful fall back if your intended campsite is a mountain bothy that might be full when you get there or you don't make it there before nightfall.

Sleeping bags
These come in many shapes, sizes, fabrics and weights. The most important feature to consider is the bag filling which gives the bag its insulating properties. There are two main types of filling: synthetic and down. Synthetic filled bags are generally cheaper, heavier and bulkier but can retain warmth when wet. Down bags are generally more expensive, lighter and pack smaller. They have the best warmth:weight ratio, but their main disadvantage is they must not be allowed to get wet, when they become almost impossible to dry and start to rapidly loose their insulation qualities. Synthetic fillings such as "hollofill" are now very advanced and approaching the qualities of down. Some bags now use a combination of synthetic and natural fillings.

Sleeping bags have a number which is based on a seasonal rating. 1-season bags are suitable for warm summer use, while 4-season bags are suitable for winter use, and 5-season bags can cope with high mountain use. The choice is baffling but if you set a budget and know the most suitable season rating for your bag you cannot go far wrong. As you may have a bag for a long time it is worth spending as much as you possibly can to ensure comfort on your expeditions. However, when choosing a sleeping bag it is important to remember that the stated insulating qualities of the bag are a guide only. Factors such as altitude, expected weather conditions and site exposure are obvious factors to help you decide.

People of different ages, sizes and outdoor experience vary greatly in what they require in terms of insulation. A one season bag can be fine for one person, but may feel uncomfortably cold to another in the same tent. If you tend to feel cold at night go for a bag with a higher season rating than you think you might need, and/or purchase some thermal sleeping wear.

The shape and size of a bag will also affect its comfort. Some bags are body-hugging "mummy style", others are rectangular in shape with more room to move about. Those with a full length zip offer greater ventilation, but will be slightly more bulky to pack. There are now women-specific sleeping bags which are slightly shorter, wider at the hips, and have extra insulation around the hood, middle and feet.

Using a sleeping bag liner made of silk or microfleece can increase insulation and help to protect the inner of your bag.

Sleeping Mats

These are very important items which will greatly improve your comfort in two ways. The first is to add a padded layer between you and the ground, and the second and more important, is to insulate you from the ground which will suck heat from you as you sleep.

Mats come in two main forms; either a closed cell foam pad, or a self-inflating open cell pad which affords more protection in both areas. The foam pad is significantly less expensive than the inflatable pad. People often compare the difference between the ground and a foam mat to the difference between a foam mat and an inflatable mat. For this reason, many people are now using inflatable mats which provide an even greater degree of comfort and insulation; the three-quarter length one is smaller and lighter than a full size foam mat and possibly more comfortable.

Stoves and cooking fuels

Food must be prepared on a small, reliable and lightweight stove which is capable of heating up quantities of food and water quickly and efficiently Stove stability, and properties and availability of the fuel the stove uses are the main things to consider when choosing a cooking system. There are three main types of stove: gas, pressurised liquid fuel and spirit stoves.

Gas stoves are the most popular type amongst the vast majority of campers as they offer a simple, clean and easily adjustable way to cook. The drawbacks are the expense and the availability of suitable gas cartridges in some remote areas. The performance of gas stoves can decrease markedly in cold conditions, and when the gas canister is getting empty. More recently, gas mixtures have gone a long way to solving some of these problems. The fuel is easy to use and burns very cleanly.

Pressure stoves are generally the most expensive but are the cheapest type of stove to run. They require a certain amount of delicate and practised handling in order to get them working, but once mastered they are very efficient, but noisy! Refuelling is not a problem no matter where you are, as many will burn on any combustible fuel such as petrol or paraffin (but not camel methane). They are reasonably controllable for simmering, but a close eye must be kept on them. The fuel must be carried in a crack-resistant container, as it is both smelly and messy.

Spirit stoves or meths burners, in particular those made by Trangia, offer a very compact and light set of stove and cooking pots in one unit and are the preferred choice for many groups of relatively inexperienced young people. The fuel is easy to use and they work well in windy conditions, an important consideration when trying to discourage people from cooking inside tents. Meths burners are cheaper than gas stoves and pressure stoves and there is also much less that can go wrong as they have no delicate moving parts. The invisible flame of a meths burner can be a hazard which has to be managed carefully. Again, carrying the fuel in a suitable crack-resistant container is essential as it can be messy.

Solid fuel stoves, the most common being the Hexamine, are little used as they require some time to heat up and do not produce any heat worthy of note. A recent development which no self-respecting expeditionist should go without occasionally is a disposable barbecue which will make you the envy of everyone else on the trip! Do be aware of the environmental impact of where you place these when lit though.

Whilst deciding which stove will suit you best do not forget the humble match or lighter as without these you best option may be reduced to the old by scout stick rubbing trick.

General kit
It is important to carry bags etc to enable rubbish to be carried out, as burning and burying is unacceptable in most areas. However, it may be important to be able to start a small fire, so matches and firelighters should be carried, especially if the intended destination for the night is a bothy. A torch is essential for the leader, and at some times of the year for all group members. It may be a good idea to have bike lights for all in case the group is delayed, and these can double up as torches.

EQUIPMENT CHECKLIST

Individual equipment	Shared equipment	Leader equipment
◊ helmet	◊ torch / bike light	◊ group first aid kit
◊ gloves	◊ map	◊ larger tool kit /
◊ warm hat	◊ compass	spares etc
◊ food / water for the	◊ stove	◊ group shelter
day	◊ spare stove seals	◊ flares / mobile
◊ whistle	◊ fuel and bottles	phone
◊ cycle shoes	◊ cooking pots	◊ Spare batteries
◊ 2 pairs socks	◊ food during camp	
◊ 2 pairs trousers /	◊ water purification	
tights / shorts	tablets	
(quick drying, so	◊ tin opener	
can be washed)	◊ pot / dishes	
◊ 2 base layers (one	cleaning kit	
can be washed	◊ toilet paper	
overnight if	◊ matches	
needed)	◊ small shovel	
◊ 2 mid layers	◊ tent	
◊ waterproof /	◊ small toolkit / spare	
breathable top	tube	
◊ toiletries	◊ insect repellent	
◊ travel towel or		
similar		
◊ sleeping bag		
◊ mug / plate / knife,		
fork		
◊ polythene bags		
◊ watch / cycle		
computer		
◊ personal 1st aid kit		

Equipment needs to be suitable for the location, weather conditions and time of year, e.g. tents that are suitable for camping in summer valleys may not be suitable for more exposed high level sites or at other times of the year. More spare clothing may need to be carried, or less, depending on conditions.

A full list of **Tools and Spares** is given in the **Bike Set-up, the Safe Cycle & Trailside Repairs** section and should be included in an expedition equipment checklist. It is important that tools are carried to fit all bikes in the group. Tools which can be shared amongst the group include: adjustable spanner, allen keys, chain tool and spare links, pliers, mole wrench, Swiss Army knife, hypercracker, spoke key and spokes (to fit each bike). Spares which should be shared amongst the group include: brake and gear cables, spare tyre, brake blocks, seat pin bolt(s), 4" bolt and nut (emergency pedal), lube, zip ties and electrical tape. When using panniers on an expedition it is well worth carrying some pannier spares in case anything breaks: spare hooks (for attaching pannier to rack), zip ties (various sizes) and spare fixing bolts for the rack.

BIKE CHECKS

All bikes should be thoroughly checked in advance of the expedition, allowing enough time for any repairs or maintenance to be carried out. When on your trip, daily checks should be carried out on each bike, paying particular attention to:

- wheels – check spokes are tight and wheels true
- brakes – check properly adjusted and replace worn blocks if necessary, check condition of brake cables
- tyres – check for bald patches, condition of tread, any damage to side walls, correct pressure of tyre
- gears – check all gears are reachable and changing smoothly, check for condition of gear cables
- bearings - check for excessive wear
- pannier rack - check all fixing bolts are tight
- chain - check for stiff links and excessive wear, lube if necessary

Making regular adjustments and carrying out maintenance after each day's ride can prevent a small problem becoming worse or in the worse case scenario a mechanical failure which could cause an accident and lead to the expedition being cut short.

CAMP CRAFT

Choosing a camp site
It is important to seek the permission and approval of the landowner before choosing any site to camp on. On arrival at the proposed venue several requirements should be considered; a camp site meeting these standards will hopefully ensure a comfortable night and a better following day's riding.

(i) Shelter
Shelter is a very important factor in allowing you a good night's sleep. Many sleepless nights have been had by people pitching tents in areas with little or no shelter. Interrupted sleep can be caused by something as trivial as the continual flutter of the tent fabric, or as major as chasing a tent around a hillside in the middle of the night. Large boulders or a wall can act as a wind break.

A block of trees provides shade in hot weather and protection from driving rain. However, do not pitch your tent directly underneath large trees. After rain has continued for a while or even after it has abated, large drips will fall on the tent which can keep you awake, and are often successful at penetrating the fly sheet. Depending on the time of year and the condition of the trees, windy weather may bring down branches from the trees, creating an obvious hazard to tents below.

(ii) Water supply

Having a good water supply close to hand is essential for cooking and for matters of personal hygiene. The supply should be free-flowing and water should be taken upstream of any suspected pollutant. If the quality of the water is at all suspect then the use of various water purifying methods is recommended. These consist of tablets, mechanical devices, and of course boiling. All water for consumption or cooking should be taken from above the area designated for personal hygiene. Great care should be taken to avoid polluting water courses with waste foodstuffs and personal hygiene items (soaps, toothpaste, washing up liquid etc).

(iii) Drainage

It is critical that your site is dry and will remain so in the event of heavy rain. Therefore choose a site which is naturally freely draining and not in a hollow. The ideal site is a slight slope which allows drainage. Do not camp in a dry river bed or a narrow valley which may be susceptible to flash flooding. Do not try to improve the drainage of a site by digging drainage channels around your tent as this is destructive to the environment.

(iv) Topography

Wherever possible avoid camping in hollows if the temperature is to be low at night. Cold air sinks below warmer air, thus hollows collect sinking cold air and could make for an uncomfortable, shivery night. For the masochists amongst you choose a boulder field but otherwise choose a site which has an even surface and is rock / pebble free.

TOILETS

Ensure that all party members are familiar with where the toilet is going to be. This is particularly important with regard to location which should be at least 60 metres from the nearest water and should always be downstream of the water supply for the camp. "Packing out" is becoming more and more common as our countryside comes under increasing pressure from recreational users. This involves removing all solid bodily waste from these areas and disposing of it in a waste bin. If this is not to be adopted then the waste should be buried at least 30 cm underground.

BITING INSECTS

Awful is the fate of the one who camps in a midge infested area during the summer months. Avoid conditions which attract dense swarms of midges – standing water, nearby cattle or sheep.

PITCHING THE TENT

When you have found a suitable area to camp, you must then pick out a specific spot within that area on which to pitch your tent. Conditions to take into account are: wind direction, cooking, and view. Quite often people will place view before wind direction as they enjoy opening the tent in the morning and having the best view possible. When rain and wind are forecast try to pitch your tent with the door in the lee of the wind to avoid rain driving through the door zips. This will also allow you to cook in the door of the tent without the tent filling with wind and taking off with you in it.

In the main, if your initial assessment of a suitable site has been good you can pitch your tent anywhere in that general location and you should remain comfortable.

When pitching a tent begin by pegging it out from the windward end and be careful to ensure that it remains neat and wrinkle free. More often than not this will only be a problem with ridge tents and is caused by over tightening guys and fly sheet pegs. It is important that you are well practiced in pitching your tent as it is significantly more difficult to pitch any tent in a howling gale than it is to pitch it on a still summer's day in your back garden. The more time you save here the drier the tent inner stays and the drier and less frustrated you will be once you've finished.

CAMP COOKING

Cooking a meal adequate for replenishing used energy and preparing the body for exercise the following day is an essential skill for the mountain bike expeditionist.

Pots and pans come in all shapes and sizes for camping. Most important is that heat is distributed evenly throughout the base of the pan so as to ensure that you use fuel most efficiently. This will get your cooking done quicker and so deliver a hot meal faster and will give you that extra brew when you need it. Cooking receptacles should also be easily washed and light and compact for transporting on your bike. If you choose non-stick items cleaning will be much easier, especially when using cold water.

Carrying three or four pots to cook with in a camp is impractical due to the implications of space available, therefore the expeditionist must be able to cook well with just one or two pots. This is possible only if you are either cooking a very basic meal or if you are well organised and you plan the order in which items should be cooked. Using old tricks such as boiling rice then leaving it while you cook the main sauce on the burner are very helpful. The rice will continue to cook and swell as long as it remains in the hot water. After the rest is cooked, finish the rice off on the burner again.

Always remember that if you can not eat all the food you cook then you should dispose of any excess. If you are conscientious this will mean packing it out twice as heavy as it was before cooking, not to mention the mess if the bag it is in bursts! Try to cook what you will eat and then cook more later if you need it. This avoids food wastage and disposal problems.

Be aware of food hygiene issues to avoid health risks associated with contaminated food or water supplies. It is best to avoid cooking meat for a group, unless it can be bought tinned or fresh locally. Remember, the "shelf-life" of any perishable foods stored in panniers will be much less than if kept in a refrigerator. Cooking only what you need will also avoid the dangers associated with re-heating foods.

The most practical ingredients for camp meals will keep well, be light to carry, and have minimal but burst-proof packaging. Porridge oats are a great carbohydrate source which will keep you going for hours. Dried fruit and nuts can be used to enrich any meal or used as snack foods throughout the day. Powdered milk and soups can be used to make an instant hot drink, or sauce for pasta or rice. There are all kinds of dried packet foods which can provide a complete meal by just adding boiling water. However, if you are camping for more than a weekend you will probably appreciate some fresh foods which may be available locally from villages or farm shops.

MISCELLANEOUS

Keeping kit dry
This in an area where people often have difficulty. It is wise to carry a few polythene bags or dry bags in which to place wet items to separate them from dry. Do not get into your sleeping bag with wet kit on as you will only succeed in getting your bag wet. This is vitally important in a down bag for reasons described earlier. Store anything that does not require to be kept dry under the fly sheet, such items include stoves, pans and water bottles.

Huts & Bothies
These are extremely useful to know about in advance when expeditioning, especially if the weather turns particularly nasty and you decide to retire to one for shelter and to allow kit to dry out. The Mountain Bothies Association welcomes cyclists at its bothies, of which there are over 100 in more remote locations across the UK www.mountainbothies.org.uk. A night in a dry, warm shelter can make all the difference to moral and boost the group's spirits before the next leg of the expedition.

Bivouacs
Planned bivouacs can be amongst the most pleasurable of expedition nights out. They allow sleeping under the stars in a controlled environment. These can only be highly recommended as multi-day options when the weather is almost guaranteed to be fair. A good Goretex or similar bivvi

bag is recommended in case of rain. Emergency and unplanned bivouacs can be very uncomfortable and can prove a very negative experience. To ensure that you will survive in relative comfort, think carefully about what you carry on your expedition by way of emergency gear. If somebody loses the tent off the back of their bike and you get to your camp site at 10 pm in the rain before you realise, could you fudge a shelter?

Fires
Before having a fire anywhere you should ensure that any landowner approves of this and when doing so you should be extremely sensitive to the environmental implications of having that fire. Ask yourself - do we really need a fire?

Emergency Repair kit
Do I have enough bits and bobs in my bike repair kit to repair a two foot rip in my fly sheet? In heavy winds this is not an uncommon occurrence and a few extra items in your bike repair kit or first aid kit would be worth their weight in gold at 4am when the tent rips.

Environmental responsibilities
Ensure that you and your companions look after the area you cycle through. This is everyone's responsibility and by doing your bit, no matter how inconsequential it may seem at the time, you can sometimes leave a site cleaner than when you encountered it. As an expedition cyclist, we should adopt a policy of minimum impact camping so as to raise the profile of mountain biking as an activity responsible for its actions.

SCOTTISH
OUTDOOR ACCESS CODE

The **Scottish Outdoor Access Code** advocates that anyone accessing the outdoors should care for the environment and help to protect the natural and cultural heritage which we enjoy. The key points of the Code with respect to wild camping are:

- Take care not to damage or disturb wildlife, vegetation or soils
- Take all litter away from your site (even if it is not yours!)
- Follow any signage aimed at protecting plants or animals, geological or archaeological features
- Do not camp or light fires on any cultural heritage site
- Help to prevent erosion by avoiding sensitive habitats such as loch shores, riverbanks, dunes and marshy ground
- Do not move, disturb or deface walls or other structures

With a little research before your trip you can find out what, if any, conservation significance an area has, not only so you are aware of any restrictions on access or permitted activities, but so you can increase your awareness of the natural and cultural interest of the area which you can share with the group.

To find out local environmental and conservation information you can contact one of the Scottish Natural Heritage Area Officers www.snh.org.uk

For more information on the Scottish Outdoor Access Code visit www.outdooraccess-scotland.com (see also the **Access** section).

On return to civilisation

Ensure that all kit is checked for damage, cleaned, dried, repaired if necessary and put away as soon as practicable after returning so that it is in a condition to be used for the next expedition, without the next user having the frustration of discovering a broken sleeping bag zip or a burn hole in the ground sheet of the tent.

Fuel & Hydration

By the end of this section leaders should be able to:

- Explain the relative importance of the three main food groups in the diet for cycling

- List good sources of carbohydrate and ways to increase carbohydrate intake

- Describe the importance of maintaining hydration and preventing dehydration

- Describe a refuelling strategy for recovery after a ride

- Demonstrate "good practice" in eating and drinking when leading a group

INTRODUCTION
It is now generally recognised that nutrition has a key role to play in influencing an athlete's ability to perform. The concept of optimal nutrition is not as clearly defined as one would imagine, though the basic concepts of good nutrition have remained strong for many years. When people are asked to define sports nutrition, often an image of pills and potions is conjured up. The truth is that optimal nutrition does *not* come in a bottle.

It is not within the scope of this manual to give a definitive guide to sports nutrition. This section will, however, give the sound building blocks of nutrition that you, as a leader and role model in mountain biking, can introduce to your groups. Correct fuelling and hydration are appropriate not only to the performance of the competitive athlete but to the enjoyment of the recreational cyclist as well, whatever their aspirations.

THE BASICS
Mountain biking is a very demanding sport, not only because of the stresses and strains it places on both your upper and lower body, but also from the energy perspective. During a mountain bike race a cyclist can expend more than 11.7kcals per minute. For a recreational cyclist this figure would be lower, however compared to many other activities, mountain biking does expend large amounts of energy.

From a practical point of view the concept of energy balance is important to everyone. This is a very simple equation; if energy consumed is equal to energy expended then a person's weight will remain stable. If the energy consumed is less than is expended then a person will lose weight. The converse happens if energy consumed exceeds requirements. This is illustrated by the diagram on the following page.

Energy Balance: Energy Eaten = Energy Expended

ENERGY FOR HEALTH AND EXERCISE

The average daily food intake should provide 2000kcal of energy for females and 2550kcals of energy for males (Department of Health, 1991). A healthy, well-balanced diet must contain the correct amounts of essential nutrients and provide adequate energy.

In terms of providing the body with fuel, carbohydrates and fats are the most significant contributors to your energy intake. Fats are the most concentrated source of energy for their given weight, providing more than double the calories per gram than carbohydrates. Fat gives 9kcals per gram, while carbohydrate and protein gives you 4 kcals per gram.

Carbohydrate is the most important fuel for the working muscles and it should make up the bulk of your diet.

The diagram below illustrates a classic experiment that was conducted to show the effect of different levels of carbohydrate on time to exhaustion. On a diet low in carbohydrate (30% of total intake), the time to exhaustion when cycling is just 1h. With moderate carbohydrate (45%) the time increases to 1h 44 minutes, while a high carbohydrate diet extends the time to 2h 50 minutes.

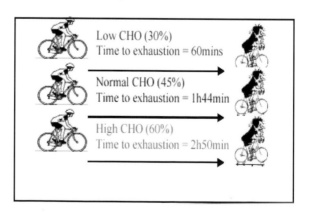

The Effect of Carbohydrate Intake on Cycling Performance

CARBOHYDRATES

Carbohydrates can be classified into two groups - sugars (simple carbohydrates) and starches (complex carbohydrates). Simple carbohydrates are sweets, sugar, glucose polymer drinks, sweet cakes and pastries. They provide an immediate burst of energy, while complex carbohydrates like potatoes, rice, pasta, vegetables, grains and pulses release their energy over a longer period of time.

Carbohydrates are stored in muscles as glycogen. The average person has approximately 2000kcals of energy stored in their muscles. When this energy source is used up it is often referred to as "hitting the wall" or the "bonk". In endurance sports like mountain biking, you can spare some of your muscle glycogen by providing an additional readily available energy source. This can be in the form of a carbohydrate snack or a carbohydrate drink.

For most sports people 60-70% of dietary energy should come from carbohydrates. In the UK the average diet contains only around 40%. As a whole, the population is being encouraged to increase the proportion of carbohydrates and reduce the amount of fat in their diet. A high carbohydrate diet is important for active people to enhance their performance as well as to improve their overall health.

The diagram below illustrates the types of foods, and the relative proportions of each, which should make up a balanced diet. Complex carbohydrates and fruit and vegetables make up the biggest parts, with smaller proportions of protein and fats.

The Balance of Good Health

GOOD SOURCES OF CARBOHYDRATE

Good sources of carbohydrate to provide energy for cycling include:

- ✓ Breakfast cereals
- ✓ Bread – all breads especially wholemeal, pitta, rolls, muffins, bagels
- ✓ Pasta – all varieties
- ✓ Rice – brown & white
- ✓ Potatoes – boiled, mashed, baked. Roast potatoes or chips are high in fat and less suitable
- ✓ All types of beans – baked, kidney, black eye, butter beans
- ✓ All pulses - lentils, peas, chickpeas, barley
- ✓ Fruit – fresh, dried or canned
- ✓ Vegetables all types – frozen or fresh
- ✓ Some cakes – although they could be high in fat. Fruit cakes or loaf, scones, gingerbread other "simple" cakes are better
- ✓ Biscuits – rich teas, plain digestive, fig rolls – rather than "fancy" biscuits
- ✓ Puddings – fruit crumbles, baked fruit, bread puddings, custard, rice pudding
- ✓ Cereals bars – some are high in fat, sports bars are best

If you are exercising regularly, and especially if you are planning an extended day's bike ride or several consecutive days biking, you should increase your carbohydrate intake in order to keep your muscles well fuelled and allow good recovery. It is often easy to underestimate the amounts of carbohydrates which have to be consumed for cycling, especially by those who are newcomers to the sport.

Below are some practical hints for increasing your carbohydrate intake.

- ✓ Eat plenty of bread and cut your slices thicker
- ✓ Try different types of bread
- ✓ Be continental by having bread with your meals as well as your rice, pasta or potatoes Add beans, chickpeas, lentils or broth mix to soups tomato sauces and salads
- ✓ Breakfast cereals are a good source of carbohydrates and can be eaten at any time of the day
- ✓ Add fresh or dried fruit to your breakfast cereal
- ✓ Snack on dried or fresh fruit, fruit scones or toast spread with jam or honey
- ✓ Make starchy foods the main items in your meal, together with plenty of fruit and vegetables

DIETARY FATS

Fat is also essential for a balanced diet. As well as providing energy it provides a medium for allowing various micronutrients into the body. Unlike glycogen, fat storage is not a limiting factor for exercise. Even the leanest of competitors has a large reserve of fat for energy, so there is no need to consume a lot of fat. You should be aiming for around 20-30% of your dietary energy to be from fat. A low-fat high-carbohydrate diet is right for both health and performance. Of your fat intake the proportion of poly- and mono-unsaturated fat (sunflower oil, PUFA margarine) should be higher than saturated fats (butter, lard, fat in meat). You should also be aware of the invisible fats in your diet, as these are the ones that are often saturated fat (e.g. cheese, meat pies, pastries, sausages, burgers, chips, crisps, fried food). Avoid hydrogenated fats as these are chemically altered and behave just like saturated fats in the body.

PROTEIN
Protein is made up of smaller building blocks called amino acids some of which can be manufactured by the body and some of which are essential and must be provided by dietary sources. Good sources of protein are meat, fish, dairy produce and pulses. One of the most common sports nutrition myths is that sports people require extra protein in their diets. The scientific evidence to date suggests that this is not the case and that the very small increase in protein requirements is easily met by the already excess protein intakes that the western world consume and therefore dietary supplementation is not required or recommended.

FLUID AND EXERCISE
Your body produces heat as a result of exercise and to dissipate this heat the body sweats. You can lose a lot of fluid by sweating and through respiration, especially if you are exercising hard and/or in hot conditions. It is especially important to be aware of this in children who might not know the importance of hydration or the symptoms of becoming dehydrated.

When the body starts to dehydrate several functions are compromised; severe dehydration results in death. **Losing even 2% of your body weight in fluid, about 1.5 kg, can impair performance by as much as 20%.** Your ability to keep riding, to co-ordinate movement and maintain concentration are all reduced with even mild dehydration. This is potentially dangerous when mountain biking and could lead to loss of control and at worst an accident.

A leader should be able to recognize the symptoms of dehydration:

> Light-headedness
> Weakness
> Nausea
> Headache
> Muscle cramps

Preventing dehydration is much easier than trying to cure it. The advice on the next page explains how to avoid dehydration occurring.

PRACTICAL ADVICE FOR STAYING HYDRATED

✓ It is vital to be well-hydrated prior to exercise – pale and plentiful urine indicates that you are well hydrated
✓ Alcohol acts as a diuretic (makes you pass more urine) so save it for post-event celebrations!
✓ Tea, coffee and cola drinks contain caffeine, which also have a diuretic effect. If you drink a lot of these you should try de-caffeinated varieties
✓ Try drinking fluid immediately before starting to cycle and continue to drink small amounts regularly throughout the ride
✓ Get used to drinking during training sessions or rides on your own and only use the drinks you are used to
✓ Thirst is *not* a good indicator of hydration – by the time you feel thirsty you are already dehydrated
✓ Remember that as soon as your ride is over you must rehydrate and begin replenishing your glycogen stores to promote good recovery

FLUID REPLACEMENT

Water is adequate fluid replacement in some situations (where sweat loss is minimal), but when sweating a lot or after a longer ride drinks containing some carbohydrate and electrolytes are better.

Suggestions for replacing fluid during and after exercise include:

✓ Water (still / mineral / plain tap water)
✓ Home-made drink: 4-8g glucose powder or glucose polymer (maltodextrin) per 100ml water + pinch of salt (to make a 4-8% solution)
✓ Fruit juice (one part) diluted with water (2 parts) with a pinch of salt
✓ Glucose polymer drink (e.g. Maxim, Hi-5, PSP, Gatorade etc)
✓ Isotonic drink (e.g. Lucozade Isotonic)

Note: it is important to observe the dilution factor when making up carbohydrate drinks, as a solution which is too concentrated will delay hydration as the body can not absorb the fluid from your stomach fast enough. For rehydration, solutions should be *no more than* 10% strength (i.e. 10g carbohydrate in 100 ml or 100g in 1 litre).

You can weigh yourself before and after exercise to see how much fluid you are losing.

Weight lost in kg X 1.5 = number of litres needed to rehydrate

For example: Pre exercise weight = 70kg
Post exercise weight = 69kg
Loss of 1kg in weight
1kg X 1.5 = 1.5 litres of fluid needed to rehydrate.

During a ride it is important to maintain hydration by having regular fluid stops, especially for less experienced riders who may not be in the habit of taking on enough fluid. As a leader you must take responsibility for ensuring everyone drinks enough to be able to cope with the day's ride and avoid the risk of dehydration. Aim to consume 1 litre each for every hour of riding, or up to 2 litres in hot weather or strenuous riding. This represents 1 large or 2 small sized water bottles or a full hydration bladder which can be worn on your back or stored in your rucksack. The latter makes taking regular sips easier, especially when mountain biking, as you only have to take one hand off the handlebars briefly. If enough fluid can not be carried for the intended duration of your ride, you must plan places where you can obtain fresh supplies.

You also need to decide if the length and demands of the route require additional fuel. This is an important consideration when leading children as their glycogen storage is considerably less than an adult's when you compare relative muscle sizes. **As a leader it is important that you maintain your own fluid and fuel intake. If you fail to do this then your concentration, perception and judgement can be impaired as a result of dehydration and fuel depletion, thus compromising your group's safety.** In summary, being properly fuelled and maintaining hydration can enhance both your and your group's enjoyment of a ride.

REFUELLING
After exercising there is a window of opportunity to refuel your muscles, often known as the "glycogen window". This window last for about 1 - 2 hours and it is when the muscles can replace glycogen (muscle carbohydrate stores) at double the rate it can normally. It is therefore very important to eat the correct foods and in the correct quantities during this time, especially when you will be riding again later in the day or the following day.

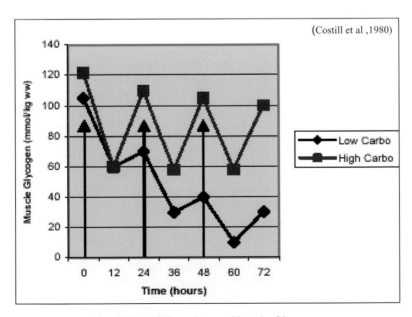

The Effect of Exercise on Muscle Glycogen

The graph on the previous page illustrates the effect of exercise on muscle glycogen. It is clear that after each period of exercise (illustrated by the black arrows) muscle glycogen is depleted. On successive days of exercise the graph shows that even with immediate and appropriate refueling (high carbohydrate) it becomes difficult to fully replenish your glycogen stores. This is why it is so important to start refuelling as soon as you can after the activity has finished. With a low carbohydrate diet the depletion of muscle glycogen is even more drastic and progressive.

If you can, it is also a good idea to top up your glycogen levels during activity. Some examples of good snacks you can eat during activity are fruit (fresh or dried), sport/ cereal bars and sandwiches. When your activity ends you should try to eat as soon as possible and practical. Often people do not feel hungry immediately after exercise as the hormone adrenaline, which is secreted during exercise, remain high for a time after exercise has. finished. However, it is important that you teach your body to accept food gradually. Foods that are high in carbohydrates and low in fat are best.

Examples of foods good for refuelling are;

- ✓ Fruit
- ✓ Fruit juice
- ✓ Sandwiches
- ✓ Breakfast cereals
- ✓ Toast
- ✓ Pasta
- ✓ Soup with bread/rolls
- ✓ Scones

GUIDELINES TO REFUELLING

Start refuelling as soon as possible after your activity has stopped. Be organised and have suitable food and drinks available at your base or in your vehicle. Carbohydrate drinks and sugary food may provide a practical and compact carbohydrate source. Small frequent meals may assist in achieving a high carbohydrate intake. Alcohol is *not* recommended to refuel the body, if you are going to consume alcohol then make sure that you have begun the refuelling process and are rehydrated first.

VITAMINS AND MINERALS

If you are eating a well-balanced healthy diet, supplementation with one or more vitamins or minerals should not be necessary. Although manufacturers claim they offer increased physical performance, prevent injuries, provide more energy or build muscles, *excess* vitamins or minerals offer no competitive edge.

There are two classes of vitamins – water soluble and fat soluble. People often imagine that if you take in extra vitamins they will do you good, or at least do you no harm. In fact, large doses of fat soluble vitamins are not eliminated from the body and can be toxic. Both classes of vitamins may cause gastro-intestinal upsets and so could potentially have a detrimental effect on your cycling.

The same advice is largely true for mineral supplementation, the possible exceptions being iron, especially in females, and minerals which are required for healthy bones (principally calcium and magnesium).

Unless you have a medical condition or an illness which has made you susceptible to vitamin or mineral deficiency, taking supplements as an "insurance policy" is not advisable. Anyone who thinks they may be suffering from a vitamin or mineral deficiency should seek medical advice, or consult a dietician who can carry out dietary analysis. Many people lack confidence that their diet is always well-balanced. Hectic lifestyles can leave little time and energy to shop, cook and eat properly. However, with a little thought and organization it should be possible to eat healthily and support a high level of activity.

PUTTING IT ALL TOGETHER

Increase your intake of carbohydrate rich foods
Bread, rice, pasta, noodles, corn, potatoes, oats, breakfast cereals, fruit and fruit juice

Eat a variety of protein foods
Lean meat, poultry, fish, pulses (peas, beans, lentils), nuts, eggs, reduced fat milk and cheese

Increase your intake of fruit and vegetables
Aim for at least 5 portions of any types of fruit or vegetable (not including potatoes)

Be properly hydrated before exercise
Thirst is a poor indicator of dehydration, so keep drinking during exercise

Rehydrate and refuel as soon as possible after exercise
Maximise recovery by consuming high carbohydrate foods and plenty of fluids

PRACTICAL TIPS FOR YOUR GROUP

Get a good breakfast
Breakfast is essential to set you up for the day. Blood sugar levels fall overnight and need to be topped up when you wake. Eating a hearty breakfast of cereals, porridge, toast, fruit and plenty of fluid will boost your energy for several hours riding.

Out on the trail
Everyone should have their own fluid supply. If the bikes have bottle cages fitted then each person should have their own bottle. This is better from a hygiene viewpoint and allows you to monitor how much each person has had to drink.

Everyone should also carry some snack food, whether that is a sandwich, muesli bar or dried fruit, even on a short ride. If an emergency occurs, returning to base could be delayed and this will lead to people getting hungry, a situation which is going to hamper your recovery plan. On longer rides or expeditions a leader must plan how much food will be required so that everybody has sufficient rations.

Setting a good example

As the leader, you are setting an example with what you choose to eat and what you do out on the trail. Out on a ride, when the leader has a drink or something to eat often the group does the same. A leader who chooses

bananas or dried fruit rather than a bar of chocolate (less good as an energy source) may influence others to do likewise. So set an example of good practice.

During your food and fluid stops you can talk about nutrition. You can explain the importance of fluids and make sure the participants are eating sufficient to provide enough energy for the day's activity. You don't have to go into great detail about diet; just highlighting the importance of nutrition and possibly talking about the importance of starchy foods like bread, potatoes, pasta and rice along with eating plenty of fruit and vegetables will get your group to think about what they are eating.

Catering

Some outdoor centres do not always have an understanding of what food is required for outdoor groups as many have come from mainstream catering. So give them a helping hand by making suggestions of what meals and snacks are suitable for your activity in advance. You can influence what is provided.

References

Bergstrom J., Hermansen L., Hultman E., Saltin B. Diet, muscle glycogen and physical performance. Acta Physiologia Scandica 1967; 71: 140-50.

Costill D.L. & Miller J.M. Nutrition for endurance sport: CHO and fluid balance. International Journal of Sports Medicine 1980; 1: 2-14.

Leadership Skills & Styles

By the end of this section all candidates should be able to:

- Describe different teaching and leadership approaches
- Describe how these approaches affect the ways in which people learn

By the end of the TCL course leaders should be able to:

- Know how to effectively apply the action centred model
- Understand some of Mosston's teaching styles and when they could *be applied*

By the end of the MBL course leaders should additionally be able to:

- Effectively apply the Hersey Blanchard situational leadership model
- Deliver a session using Mosston's teaching styles

INTRODUCTION

It is suggested that if we develop understanding of different ways of presenting information and technical content then our ability to cater for all learners will be greatly increased. As such, the quality of teaching will improve and our leadership style will be appropriate to the situation. As Leaders, these are things that we should constantly strive towards.

WHAT IS A LEADER?

A Leader is someone who exercises a definite and particular role in relation to others

A Role is a set of expected behaviours associated with a position in a group

A leader will have a range of skills or general functions specifically pertinent to effective leadership. The more important of these are:

- responsibility
- control
- care
- support
- setting and maintenance of standards and limits
- decision making
- sustaining the group's energy
- engagement and commitment of personal energy to the group's aims
- awareness of and responsiveness to one's own feelings, wants and needs, and those of the group as individuals and as a whole

To carry out these functions effectively a leader needs to be able to call on a range of both technical and relationship skills. The technical skills are presented in the other modules of this manual. Some of the more important "people skills" are trainable and can be acquired to assist the leader in performing their role. These skills should be developed from conscious skills into ingrained habits.

LEADERSHIP QUALITIES

Leading and teaching skills can be viewed along a spectrum, where at one end all responsibility rests with the leader, and at the other end, decision making is devolved to the learner. As the relationship between the leader and group develops it becomes possible, sometimes necessary or desirable, for the leader to use alternative ways of exercising control.

The leader has to decide which particular approach to use. Leadership is an interactive, two-way process involving both the leader and the learner in decision making and responsibility.A leader requires a wide range of competencies to fulfil the role successfully. The Leadership Competencies list on the following page shows a "top 10" of the skills, behavioural qualities and knowledge which candidates felt were important to the role of Trail Cycle Leader. Candidates on a training course will be asked to fill in a similar sheet . An example of a skill might be "Navigation", behaviour/ qualities might be "calm in a crisis" and knowledge might include "awareness of access issues".

SKILLS	BEHAVIOUR/ QUALITIES	KNOWLEDGE
Planning	People Skills	Underpinning Knowledge
Bike Skills	Patience/Tolerance	Health and Safety
Navigation	Motivational	Routes and Terrain
Teaching	Sense of Humour	Weather
Organisational	Confidence	Research
Delegation	Empathy/Compassion	Group Dynamics
Decision Making	Observant	Access
Communication	Good listener	Conservation
Group Control/ Management	Flexibility	Emergency Procedures
Emergency repairs	Judgement	Hazard Awareness
First Aid	Trust	Repairs
Teambuilding	Self Discipline	Risk Assessment
Goal Setting	Responsibility	Escape Routes
Incident Management	Assertiveness	Leadership Styles
Judgement	Calm in Crisis	Fitness
Motivation	Sense of Fun	Nutrition
	Time Management	Clothing
	Sensitivity	Local Routes
	Problem Solving	N.G.B.
	Well Prepared	Natural History
	Diplomatic	Working with Children
	Honesty	Highway Code
		Environmental Protection
		Setting up Bike
		Relevant Legislation
		Flora/Fauna
		Bike Maintenance
		Local History
		Local Geography
		Cadence
		First Aid
		Rules/Bye-laws

LEADERSHIP MODELS

There are a number of leadership models which have been used in leadership training. They have become more generally known in outdoor activities since the late 1970's. They are helpful and useful as aids to help leaders to think and develop their own ideas about leadership.

Two models of leadership are described; you will be introduced to one at each level (TCL and MBL) of the award. The first one, "The Action Centred Leadership Model", is included as an early aid for Trail Cycle Leaders. Generally, inexperienced "leaders", "coaches" and "teachers" can easily focus most of their attention on the task rather than on other leadership functions.

TCL

LEADERSHIP MODEL 1 – The Action Centred Leadership (TCL)

John Adair suggests that the three main aspects a leader will constantly have to keep in mind and cope with to achieve a particular task are:-

- The Task
- The Team
- The Individual

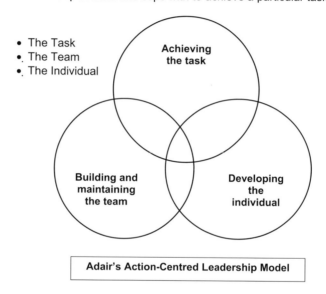

Achieving the task

Building and maintaining the team

Developing the individual

Adair's Action-Centred Leadership Model

This model should be used following a period of leadership to check where the leader's focus of attention has been. Over a period of time (e.g. a half or whole day session) it would be expected that a leader would spread their focus between the task, the team and the individual.

All three areas should be regarded as interlinked in that an over-concentration on one will be to the detriment of the other two. For example, a single-minded concentration by the leader on the task is likely to result in a breakdown of communication with the group. Conversely, concentrating too much on individuals within the group could mean that the attainment of the group's goal is put in jeopardy or never achieved.

This model provides one way for the leader to identify and decide which of the three areas most requires immediate attention in a working situation.

The following checklists are designed to help apply the 3 areas of the leader's responsibility.

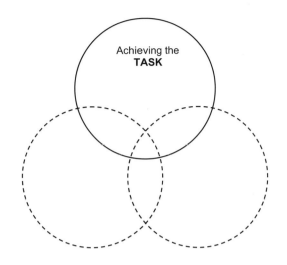

TASK

Purpose:	Am I clear what the task is?
Responsibilities:	Am I clear what mine are?
Objectives:	Have I agreed these with the person accountable for the group?
Programme:	Have I worked one out to reach objectives?
Working Conditions:	Are these right for the job?
Resources:	Are these adequate?
Targets:	Has each member clearly defined and agreed them?
Authority:	Is the line of authority clear?
Training:	Are there any gaps in the specialist skills or abilities of individuals in the group required for the task?
Priorities:	Have I planned the time available?
Supervision:	In case of my absence who covers for me?
Example:	Do I set standards by my behaviour?

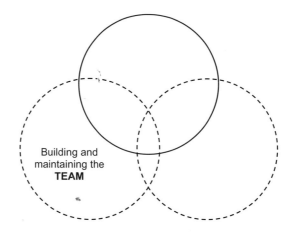

TEAM

Objectives: Does the team clearly understand and accept them?

Standards: Do they know what standards of performance are expected?

Safety Standards: Do they know the consequences of infringement?

Size of Team: Is the team size correct?

Team Members: Are the right people working together? Is there a need for subgroups to be formed?

Team Spirit: Do I look for opportunities for building teamwork into jobs? Do methods of instruction help to develop team spirit?

Discipline: Are the rules seen to be reasonable? Am I fair and impartial in enforcing them?

Grievances: Are grievances dealt with promptly? Do I take action on matters likely to disrupt the group?

Consultation: Is this genuine? Do I encourage and welcome ideas and suggestions?

Briefing: Is this regular? Does it cover current plans, progress and future developments?

Representation: Am I prepared to represent the feelings of the group when required?

Support: Do I encourage individuals when the team is not working well together?

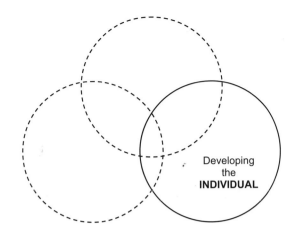

Developing
the
INDIVIDUAL

INDIVIDUAL

Targets: Have they been agreed and quantified?

Achievement: Does he/she know how his/her work contributes to the overall result?

Responsibilities: Has he/she got a clear and accurate job? Can I delegate more to him/her?

Authority: Does he/she have sufficient authority for his/her task?

Training: Has suitable training been provided ?

Recognition: Do I emphasise people's successes? In failure, is criticism constructive?

Growth: Does he/she see the chance of development? Does he/she see some pattern of improvement?

Reward: Are work, capacity and reward in balance?

The person: Do I know the person well? What makes him/her different from others?

Time/Attention: Do I spend enough time with individuals, listening, developing, counselling?

Grievances: Are these dealt with promptly?

Security: Does he/she know about safety arrangements?

Appraisal: Is the overall performance of each individual regularly reviewed?

OBSERVATION OF THE LEADER

One way of helping course members develop their awareness of leadership behaviour is to review a session after someone has been leading the group. Imagine there are 100 points to be allocated amongst the three overlapping circles. How many points would be allocated to each one?

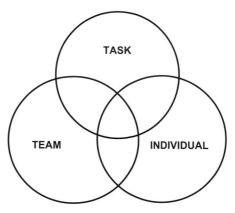

If the leader focussed largely on one task to the exclusion of the other two areas, most of the points would be allocated there. If there was equal emphasis then the points should be spread more evenly between the three circles. Reviewers should be able to justify their allocation of points by giving clear examples of how the task was achieved, how each individual was developed and how the team was built and maintained.

During a period of leadership, all three areas would be expected to have received a balance of the leader's attention.

ASSESSING LEADERSHIP ABILITY

An attempt has been made to create a tool for assessing leadership competence. This was prepared for the SMBLA when it began mapping TCL competencies to National Occupational Standards. The table on the following two pages is set out in that style, where the unit of "leadership" is

expanded into 6 key elements. Each element has performance criteria which should be achieved before the unit of leadership can be passed. This work is presented to assist in understanding of the leadership competence required to undertake any leadership role whether it is on a bike or under other circumstances.

LEADERSHIP ELEMENTS	PERFORMANCE CRITERIA
1. Managing a Group Safely and Effectively	1. Obtains sound relationship 2. Takes sensible decisions on safety 3. Keeps control 4. Keeps everyone informed 5. Keeps in touch with whole group
2. Making Decisions	1. Considers all relevant factors 2. Doesn't avoid difficult/unpopular decisions 3. Listens to opinions when relevant 4. Is decisive when required 5. Consults as appropriate
3. Setting and Maintaining Standards	1. Establishes ground rules 2. Enforces ground rules 3. Leads by example
4. Using a Range of Styles	1. Selects style appropriate to circumstances 2. Exhibits use of range of styles
5. Showing Concern for the Group	1. Reach agreement on objectives 2. Encourage group to work together 3. Involve everyone 4. Control the group
6. Achieving the Task	1. Be successful in achieving objective 2. Work to the plan 3. Take the whole group along 4. Keep to time

LEADERSHIP MODEL 2 – Situational Leadership (MBL)

For years, when people talked about leadership style, they identified two extremes – an autocratic (directive) leadership style and a democratic (supportive) leadership style. Autocratic leaders used position, power and their authority to get results, while democratic leaders used personal power and involved others in participative problem-solving and decision-making processes.

Hersey and Blanchard in "Leadership and Administration of Outdoor Pursuits" by Phyllis Ford and James Blanchard (1985), tell us that the continuum between human relationships and the accomplishment of tasks, one's leadership style, will depend on two variables: the *level of maturity* of the group of followers and the *demands of the situation*.

The *demands of the situation* relate to the task to be accomplished. In outdoor pursuits the situation may range from formal to informal, tense to relaxed, dangerous to safe. It may demand a great amount of leader control or little or no control.

Situation demands little leader control	Situation needs some leader control	Situation demands complete leader control
Cycling in playground, checking that bike gears are working	Cycling at moderate speeds along an easy trail	Descending a steep rocky section of single track trail

Further research showed that leadership styles tend to vary considerably from situation to situation, and that it is not helpful to think of leadership style as an *either/or* continuum. While the behaviour of some leaders is characterised mainly by directing their followers' activities in terms of task accomplishment (directive behaviour), other leaders concentrate on providing socio-emotional support and on building personal relationships between themselves and their followers (supportive behaviour). In other situations, various combinations of directive and supportive behaviour are evident. Thus, it was determined that directive and supportive leader behaviours are not either/or leadership styles. Instead, these patterns of leader behaviour can be plotted on two separate and distinct axes.

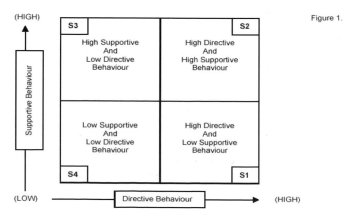

Figure 1.

DIRECTIVE AND SUPPORTIVE LEADER BEHAVIOURS

MBL

Directive behaviour is defined as:
the extent to which a leader engages in one-way communication; spells out the follower(s) role and tells the follower(s) what to do, where to do it, when to do it and how to do it; and then closely supervises performance.

Three words can be used to define directive behaviour: structure, control, supervise.

Supportive behaviour is defined as:
the extent to which a leader engages in two-way communication, listens, provides support and encouragement, facilitates interaction and involves the follower(s) in decision making.

Three words can be used to define supportive behaviour: praise, listen and facilitate.

In *style 1* (S1) (figure 1.) a leader is high on direction, low on support. He/she defines roles and goals, provides specific instruction to the follower(s), and closely supervises task accomplishment. When using *style 2* (S2) the leader is high on both direction and support. He or she explains decisions and solicits suggestions from the follower(s), but continues to direct task accomplishment. *Style 3* (S3) leader behaviour is characterised by high supportive low directive behaviour. The leader and follower(s) make decisions together and then the leader supports the followers' efforts toward task accomplishment. In *style 4* (S4), a leader provides low support and direction. He or she turns over decisions and responsibility for implementation to the follower(s)

Styles of Leadership
Each of the four leadership styles outlined above can be identified with a different approach to problem solving and decision making as illustrated by the diagram below.

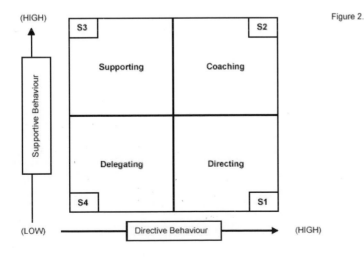

Figure 2.

The styles of leadership model explanations are amended and reproduced with the author's permission from "Leading and Managing Groups in the Outdoors", by Ken Ogilvie.

S1- Directing High directive/Low supportive leader behaviour
This style is well illustrated in the early stages of a group's life when the members are uncertain of each other, not too sure about the leader and a bit hazy about the objective. The important thing is to get the task moving by feeding in much information and perhaps imparting a lot of skill. In this

situation the leader will be doing a lot of telling and directing and staying in charge. Personal feelings and group needs will be secondary to the achievement of the task. Emergencies would come into this category. The maturity (development stage) of the group is low and the leader may well have a very impersonal relationship with the group.

S2 – Coaching High directive/High supportive leader behaviour
In this situation the leader will be active and visible but not necessarily directive. A lot is going on, such as in the "early" phase of a new group's life. Questions to do with 'why' rather than 'what' are being asked, so reasons and explanations are required in order to persuade and convince e.g. Why do we have to go up this trail rather than down that one?

Good relationships are as important as getting on with the job because at this juncture if the relationship becomes soured the task may not be achieved. At this stage the leader's role tends to become political and diplomatic in essence, particularly when conflicts, a feature of this phase, have to be resolved positively. In other words, to be effective, the leader has to be flexible in order to be able to adapt to a variety of conditions or situations. The sustained exercise of a single leadership style here might well be disastrous.

S3 – Supporting High Supportive/Low directive leader behaviour
Here, roles have been assigned to, or assumed by, group members with the skills and ability to undertake them. Control of some things is moving naturally away from the leader. But it is important that, with the removal of this cohesive influence, group harmony is maintained so that various parts continue to work together. In order not to become too distant from the group, it is now possible for the leader's focus to move away from the task, and concentrate more on the needs and wants of the group and individuals within it. The leader will thus participate on a level nearer to the group by joining, sharing, testing and consulting. On some expeditions leadership never gets beyond this phase because of a leader's need to feel that his/her group remain dependant. This is a limited view and can be considered as unjust or selfish in that it blocks the development of others.

S4 – Delegating Low supportive/Low directive leader behaviour
In this situation the leader allows his/her role to become low key in order that the group is able to become self functioning to the extent that it, or individuals in it, can see what needs to be done, set up tasks, take most of the decisions and carry them out. The leader will be mostly delegating, consulting a little, supervising a lot and monitoring all the time. A physical example of this sort of situation would be a group well on the way to self sufficiency as say with an established, fairly well trained and experienced group, preparing to go on a semi-accompanied expedition as part of the training for the Duke of Edinburgh Award Scheme.

There is a possibility of becoming confused here: within the expedition group there will need to be high supportive behaviour in order to carry out a task that may be simple at times and complex at others. So how does this fit into a category of Low supportive/Low directive behaviour? The distinguishing feature here is that the relationship between leader and the group needs to be less involved.

Relating situational demands to group maturity or development tells us that the leader's style will change depending on the task/relationship orientation as well as group maturity.

To further illustrate the four dimensions above, assume a group of adults is starting their first mountain-biking excursion. As a whole, the group's knowledge, skills, and ability to take responsibility for itself is very limited (immature), and safety is a prime concern of the leader who would use a directive approach with little interaction with the learners. However, leadership style would change to a point where it might even be participative, as the learners develop their skills and maturity in the activity and become as adept as their leader.

Some leaders' own behaviour may be 'locked' at the outer edge of the two axes in figure 1. In other words, leaders who 'need' to be 'in charge' at all times may find it uncomfortable to develop a 'supportive behaviour' role. Similarly, some teachers may find it hard to take control and this may not be advantageous in certain situations where safety is an issue.

There are some psychometric tests which can be used to determine a leader's comfort zone and some people require to make a considerable effort to operate as a well rounded leader who considers and achieves group development, as well as task achievement.

TEACHING MODELS

The aim of this section is to consider teaching "approaches" or "styles". It may be appreciated that an effective teacher adopts a flexible approach in common with an effective leader. The skilled teacher will use judgement and experience to decide how much responsibility to delegate and when the time is "right" to do so.

Whilst quality demonstration, analysis of performance, selection of terrain, and good clear management are vital skills to possess, so too is the ability to teach using various "approaches" or "styles" and to constantly evaluate the success of each style used with both individuals and groups.

In all forms of modern education, the emphasis is increasingly on encouraging a more participative approach, with students becoming actively involved in learning. This section will focus on the work of a noted American Physical Educationalist, Muska Mosston. He has provided a model for studying teaching approaches which offers a useful framework for our purpose. This framework is known as "Mosston's Spectrum of Teaching Styles". Many national governing bodies of sport have now adopted Mosston's teaching styles as the basis for their coach education programmes.

One important area we are not directly considering is how individuals will learn. There are vast differences in how individuals learn, some are much more receptive to auditory signals, others are predominately visual learners, whilst some learn most through active practice. Also, most individuals learn differently under different circumstances and at different times. By being able to teach or lead in a range of styles, leaders can greatly improve their chances of success with most individuals.

In his work Mosston makes it clear that each of his eight styles possesses key features and particular strengths and weaknesses. The spectrum is not presented as a hierarchy of style, and one is not necessarily better than any other. The best style is the one which will be most effective for the learners during any particular teaching episode.

Spectrum of Styles

A	B	C	D	E	F	G	H
●	●	●	●	●	●	●	●
Command	Practise	Reciprocal	Self Check	Inclusion	Convergent	Divergent	Learner Designed Programme

THE ESSENCE OF EACH STYLE

Style A – "Command Style" In this style, the teacher directs the members of his/her class in all their actions; a clear comparison being possible with a sergeant major controlling a group of recruits on a barracks square.

Key Features of the Command Style are:
To learn to perform a task accurately and efficiently. It provides for teacher control and learner compliance. The learner does not take any active decisions except consenting to take part.

Implications

TCL
&
MBL

- Subject matter is fixed, a single standard to be followed.
- The teacher's demonstration of the skill establishes the model to be copied.
- The teacher's commands must be obeyed with great care in performance.
- The teacher's decisions cannot be questioned.
- Individual differences in the abilities of learners cannot be taken into consideration.

Style B – "Practice Style" This style enables the teacher to provide the class with a model of performance, probably by demonstration, which the student then tries, with repetition, more or less at their own pace. It is perhaps the style of teaching most frequently employed by teachers of physical activities particularly when introducing a new technique.

Key Features of the Practice Style are:
It provides for near maximum opportunity to practise the task at hand and to receive feedback individually and privately.

Implications
- Students learn to make certain (not all) decisions about performance and to accept the consequences of those decisions.
- They learn to perform tasks within constraints of time and space.
- They learn to accept private and individual feedback.

Style C – "Reciprocal Style" In this style the teacher divides the class into pairs, whose members work together as "performer" and "observer" in turn, providing each other with immediate feedback according to clear criteria provided by the teacher.

Key Features of the Reciprocal Style are:
By working co-operatively, partners provide each other with immediate, one-to-one feedback. Evaluation of the performance of a skill/activity are shifted from teacher to learner who observes a partner's performance and also provides feedback on the basis of criteria laid down by the teacher.

Implications
- This style promotes a new kind of relationship among learners.
- Patience and tolerance are developed and exhibited.
- Reciprocation of giving and receiving feedback is developed and exhibited.
- Precision in offering feedback by criteria is developed.

- Learning the task itself is facilitated due to immediate feedback from the partner.
- The teacher can stand back and monitor the work of the observers as well as the developments of the whole group.

Style D – "Self-Check Style" Whilst operating in this style, the teacher enables the class or group to work individually to analyse and reflect upon their own performance. However, the correct direction and guidelines are still provided by the teacher.

Key Features of the self-check style are:
The self-check style provides opportunities for self-assessment. By a further shift in decision making, a situation is created in which the learners' skills in analysing performance are enhanced, and they are required to apply those skills to analyse their own performance rather than that of a learning partner.

Implications
- Learners expand their experience in working privately.
- They learn to "feel" and "sense" their own performance.
- They learn to use criteria to improve their own performance.
- They learn to be honest and objective about their own performance.
- They learn about discrepancies and their own limitations.
- They learn to be more independent of the teacher as the sole source of feedback.
- There is more individualising than in previous styles. Learners make individual decisions about themselves both in the "performance" and "reflective" phase.

Style E – "Inclusion Style" In this style learners are again allowed to operate individually, but are provided with more opportunities for selecting the level at which they attempt a particular activity; more or less demanding according to choice.

Key Features of the Inclusion Style are:
The Inclusion Style provides the opportunity for each learner to be included in the task at hand. In each of the styles identified so far, the task had been thought of in terms of a single standard and no consideration has been

given to individual differences amongst learners. Up to this point, the teacher has the opportunity to alter the nature of the feedback in accordance with the learners' performance but this does not alter the fact that learners have been working towards a teacher-determined level of performance. Style E addresses this problem which is of crucial importance to all teachers.

Implications
- The learner is given the opportunity to select a standard that suits his/her abilities.
- The teacher's main task is to ensure that there is a sufficient range of options available.
- Opportunity is provided to choose the standard of performance where success can be "guaranteed".
- There is the opportunity to take a step backward in order to succeed in the activity.
- There are options to move on if one wishes to do so.
- Promotes learning of self-assessment and deals with the (frequent) discrepancy between aspiration and reality.

Style F – "Guided Discovery" (Convergent Style) Here, the success of the style rests on the effectiveness of the teacher in asking questions of the learner or learners. The questions may be posed verbally or by setting problems, but should result in the learners reaching a similar conclusion to the teacher, "converging" in their thinking.

Key Features of the Guided Discovery Style are:
None of the styles identified so far have made significant demands of learners in terms of their ability to understand and think more deeply about performance, rather they have been concerned with reproduction of knowledge as given by the teacher. To develop situations wherein learners have a different relationship to that knowledge, Mosston claims that learners have to go beyond the discovery threshold. The first of two styles (F and G) which takes learners beyond this discovery threshold is based on the notion of "guided discovery" and the process of CONVERGENT THINKING.

Performance: teacher presents a situation to create a thinking process in the learner which, when resolved, becomes subject matter (e.g. "Which is the more effective brake on a bike?")

Evaluation: when feedback information is fundamental to the task, the learner can evaluate their own responses, otherwise the teacher provides the feedback.

Style F is dependant on the teacher's skill in asking appropriate questions, in sequence, during the performance phase.

Implications
- Develops a precise relationship between the learner's response and the stimulus (questions presented by the teacher).
- Develops a relationship between the teacher and the learners which is based on discovery by a learner (this is fundamentally different from the stimulus–response relationship that occurs in the Command Style A).

- Develops sequential discovery skills that logically lead to the discovery of a concept.
- Develops the patience (in both teacher and learner) required during the discovery process.

Style G – "Divergence Style" While the teacher still poses the question or sets the problem in this style, in contrast with the previous (Convergent) style, the answer or answers may be varied and unexpected. In others words, the learner is required to both understand more and be more creative than previously.

Key Features of the Divergence Style are:
This style of teaching is based on the process of divergent thinking. The shift in decision making which identifies this style of teaching is outlined as:

Performance: learners create subject matter by discovering alternative solutions to questions posed by the teacher (e.g. cornering on bike)

Evaluation: depending on subject matter, learner verifies own solutions or receives feedback from the teacher

This style requires the teacher to consider and use something called the "PFD reduction process", which can be defined as, "the successive use of criteria to reduce a given number of solutions". For example, is a particular day's ride possible for a given group given the constraints of fitness, terrain, weather, time of year, equipment, group skill etc? Is it feasible with the time available? Is it the "best" and most rewarding route for the group?

PFD Reduction

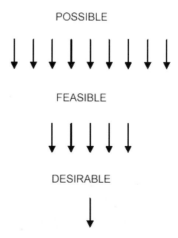

Implications
- To tap the thinking capacities of the teacher in designing problems in a given subject matter area.
- To tap the thinking capacities of the learners in discovering multiple solutions to any given problem.

- To develop insight into the nature of the activity and discover possible variations.
- To reach the level of effective security which "permits" the teacher and the learner to go beyond accepted responses, i.e. to go beyond the conventional.
- To develop the ability to confirm solutions and test them in context.

Style H – "Learner Designed Programme" Although the teacher may still prescribe the general area of enquiry for the learner or learners, it would be up to the learners to identify the specific problem to be solved or design the programme to be followed. Perhaps, if they wish, they could call upon the teacher for advice, guidance or even direct instruction.

This style requires the learner to use the skill and understanding developed earlier, and apply them in a context in which work is undertaken much more independently of the teacher. In style H the learner identifies the questions or problems prescribed by the teacher.

The style, which can only be followed over a series of episodes, is dependant on the learner having a sound understanding of the subject matter. Only then can the learner identify relevant questions in a highly disciplined manner and thus avoid the situation in which "anything goes".

Style H provides opportunities for students to develop initiative and be guided and reminded, if necessary, during the progress of a self-motivated project. The main limitation is that the project has to be undertaken within the parameters of the teacher's knowledge, conditions, time etc.

SUMMARY
Styles and their use have to be judged on how appropriate they are. Decisions about their suitability can only be made by the teacher whilst taking into account:

- Maturity of the learner
- Nature of the activity (complexity, danger element)
- Confidence/competence of the teacher

Expectations of the learner in terms of how the teacher will operate are a significant factor in any teacher/learner situation. It is important, therefore, that the respective roles are clarified before any teaching episode begins and re-enforced as the episode progresses.

Research has shown that "Spectrum" Teachers display the following qualities:

- Exhibit flexibility in different use of styles
- Give more individual attention to students
- Spend less time dominating discussions
- Use time more efficiently, evidenced by:
  - students pay more attention
  - more time is spent on work
  - less time is spent on distractions
  - less time is spent on discipline
  - more subject matter is taught

And "Spectrum" Students show corresponding characteristics:

- greater flexibility in coping with learning demands
- more independence and responsibility
- posses a clearer idea of tasks and roles

APPLICATION OF VARIOUS TEACHING STYLES (MOSSTON) IN THE TEACHING OF MOUNTAIN BIKING

The following is intended to provoke thought among those teaching and leading mountain bike groups.

A Command Style
Suitable for the following:

- Teaching basic skills such as setting up a safe bike or braking
- Leading in hazardous positions on, for example, a steep slope
- Coping with an unforeseen crisis

B Practice Style
May be employed to gain maximum class activity when the class size is large or the range of abilities is great. The class may be split so that each part may try an appropriate manoeuvre. Suitable for teaching, for example:

- In a wide area, use of gears
- Attempting to manoeuvre round obstacles

C Reciprocal Style
Useful at a stage when it is desirable to increase analytical skill, e.g. for aspiring leaders. Pairs can work on "bunny hops" or some other technical aspect, where one or two clear "points for observation and feedback" are used. Simple instructions on cards could be useful here.

D Self Check
Individuals can work on refining own skills as determined by the teacher.

- Body positioning on steep descent or ascents
- Braking without skidding

E The Inclusion Style
Programme level is determined by choice of each learner. For example, ascent or decent of a bank where there is choice in selecting the slope angle and length.

F Guided Discovery
Employs the use of exercises to assist in discovering "correct" position on the bike, or technique to be used.

- Selection of gears for optimum performance
- Determining which is the more effective brake (front or rear)
- Climbing a steep slope (body position)

G Divergent
Students make, for example, choices over equipment, line of slope, type of turns, speed etc. Decisions are made according to equipment, experience,

fitness, conditions etc. They choose the route for the day, length of outing and type of terrain.

H Individual Programme Student's Design

Learner has achieved almost total independence. Learner decides how he/she wishes to use expertise of the teacher or trainer, and may seek assistance when required. For example, a trainee racer may decide the type of discipline and even the training schedule, possibility with advice from a trainer. Advice from the teacher on which area, trails and types of terrain offer the greatest challenge, as well as the greatest aesthetic rewards.

CONCLUSION

The role of teacher or leader can be particularly challenging, and carrying out this role effectively is vital. Initially there is likely to be the desire to operate in a "command" style of teaching and the similar "directing" style of leadership. As confidence and experience grow, the teacher/leader is likely to experiment with the ranges of "styles" outlined in this section. Such experimentation is normal and should be evaluated for effectiveness. Eventually, the complete range of styles should be well within the repertoire of skills which the effective leader can employ. As more and more responsibility is undertaken by group members and as their skills develop, the leader must avoid "holding on" and recognise that such a development can be considered the result of effective instruction.

Planning & Group Management

By the end of this section Leaders should be able to:-

- Describe the types of prior knowledge required of a group leader about the group

- Describe how this knowledge might be put to use in planning a group session

- Understand the Leader:Group size ratio from an insurance and advisory perspective

- Answer the question, "What are the aims of this group"? for each group being led

INTRODUCTION

Riding bikes off-road and away from the inherent risks and conflicts with traffic is an excellent opportunity to draw a broad cross section of society into cyclesport and to allow them to engage with the outdoors in an exciting and accessible way. It promotes the use of urban as well as remote environments and allows the benefits of an 'outdoor activity' to cross over into the everyday lives of participants. To ride a bike can be a spiritual and enjoyable experience as much as it can be an extreme sport or a pathway to elite fitness and competition.

1. THE GROUP

To operate as successful leaders of groups it is fundamental that we recognise the wide range of abilities, expectations and responses our students have to the challenges of cycling. It would be imprudent to expect a BMX racer to have the same expectations from a session as someone who has ridden a bike only twice in the last year, for example. Within every group of young people or adults the combination of fitness, experience and skills makes an inclusive and enjoyable session hard to achieve. A skilled Trail Cycle Leader or Mountain Bike Leader could find themselves employed to run a taster session in a forest park for a local school one day and guiding well equipped and very skilled recreational riders the next. The delivery repertoire of the award

holder must flex to meet the very different needs of each client group. In order to achieve this, the following section sets out a list of important ingredients that come together to make for a successful off-road session.

Prior knowledge

To have knowledge of the needs and abilities of your groups is a fundamental starting point for the session plan that follows. To have in your possession documented participant information which includes names, ages, addresses, next of kin, any medical issues and the background of your group (youth/school/leisure) makes an adequate starting point. You also need to ascertain the same personal information for any accompanying staff and leaders. The medical information of a 50 year old sedentary classroom teacher is as important to the party leader as the 14 year old(s) he or she is responsible for.

In order to deliver the outcomes of the session to an acceptable standard the leader also needs background knowledge of the group's expectations and any outcomes requested by the sponsor. Is the session fitted into a framework of a residential personal development course? Is it tied into training for the Duke of Edinburgh Award or are the group expecting a challenging ride designed to develop their off-road riding skills?

Armed with the group's expectations it is now a good idea to assess their abilities and entry behaviour to the session. Do their expectations outweigh their abilities? At what point does adventure become misadventure for a group of novices wanting to ride technical singletrack, or at the other end of the spectrum are the group of skilled adventure racers going to get sufficient stimulation riding the local towpaths?

Group Size

"What is the ideal group size ?" is always a difficult question to answer. Leader:Group ratios must be based on risk assessment and take into account prior knowledge as discussed in this section (age, ability, expectations, weather, time of year etc).

 SMBLA Leader ratios would not normally exceed 1:8. This would require a Leader to be covered by their employer's insurance, which may be a Local Authority. **If a Leader is depending on British Cycling insurance through Silver or Gold membership the maximum ratio is 1:6.**

Two leaders to a group of 12-16 participants gives a workable situation for most outdoor centres. To work with larger groups than this can cause its own problems; educational and development agendas can be hard to deliver as 'crowd control' becomes the order of the day. The impact on other trail users and the environment is increased with larger group sizes and effective management is impaired.

Equipment

What to carry on an off-road cycling venture can be a topic for much discussion and the finer points and preferences will largely depend on the type of journey and the terrain to be crossed. A leader must issue a "what to bring" list to his/her group in advance, and make plans to borrow or hire equipment which individuals can not provide. The "what to bring" list can also act as a check list to use before the ride.

Below is a minimum list of equipment broken down into leader, group and personal equipment lists. For a day journey it is assumed that all equipment will be carried in a small rucksack or similar. See the **Expedition Planning** section for more information on equipment needs for an extended self-supported trip.

Leader equipment (in addition to personal equipment)
◊   Adequate tool kit, to include:
Multi-tool or equivalent
Tyre levers
Puncture repair kit
Spare Tubes (X2 with presta type valves)
Pump
Chain tool
Zip Ties (various)
Spoke Key(s)
Chain Lube
Tyre Boot or Patch
Superglue
Crank extractor
Adjustable spanner
Knife
Duck Tape
Brake pads/blocks
◊   First aid kit
◊   Compass
◊   Whistle
◊   Map (and waterproof case)
◊   Mobile phone
◊   Head torch
◊   Polythene Survival Bag
◊   Spare warm clothing (for group members)
◊   Emergency food
◊   Extra fluids

Personal items
◊   Helmet
◊   Gloves
◊   Eye protection
◊   Windproof/Waterproof jacket
◊   Suitable footwear
◊   Clothing to fit the environment/season
◊   Food
◊   Drink
◊   Medication (inhalers etc)

Group equipment
◊   Emergency Group Shelter
◊   Extra spares for longer / more remote trips (pedals, tyre, cables etc)

Fitness

Cycling off-road places a different set of demands on the body to many other activities and it is of primary importance that any planned session operates within the abilities of the group. When a cycling group becomes energy depleted their concentration and skill on the bike will suffer with a corresponding effect on their safety. Also, an exhausted group will become more prone to cold injury (potentially leading to hypothermia) and will become debilitated very quickly.

The endurance fitness so critical to cycling is something that develops over years of riding and it is easy for a leader to underestimate the physical challenges experienced by their group. Sessions should be progressive with plenty of time allowed for refuelling and resting. Strategies for managing disparity of fitness levels in the group should be prepared and routes planned should not be considered without taking account of the ability of the weakest member.

Aspirations

It is a commonly held belief that everyone can ride a bike. This misconception both helps and hinders the Trail Cycle / Mountain Bike Leader. It gives confidence and encourages young people into the activity but it can allow members of groups to ride in an unsafe way whilst under instruction and leadership. Before embarking on a cycling session it is important that a leader evaluates his plans against the stated aims of the session. This gives perspective and rigour to the plan and checks that the aspirations of the leader are in tune with the outcomes for the group. I might like to ride miles of sinuous single track but is that the right experience for a group working on gear selection and cadence during their first sessions of a programme? The aspirations of the leader must match the abilities of the group whilst in his/her charge. If there is a mismatch in this partnership then the group will experience de-motivating difficulty or even injury if the goals of the leader are too high, or boredom if the leader's plans do not provide enough challenge.

2. AIMS

The sections in this manual that address teaching and leadership focus on providing some form of cycling activity. Whether that activity involves providing an experience of the outdoors, allowing a process of personal development or increasing the skills of a mountain biker, one thread underlies all. Each session delivered by a Mountain Bike Leader or Trail Cycle Leader must have an aim. To have an aim in mind when planning a session allows outcomes to be judged, it allows focus and should give direction to the experience provided. "Why am I doing this?" should be the first question a leader asks themselves before planning their session. If the answer is "I don't know" then an alarm bell should start to ring! As leaders on mountain bikes we have responsibility to our clients. If we can't focus on their basic needs then we don't merit the opportunity to take the job on.

Some aims will be consistent in each session run. "To provide a safe and enjoyable session" for example would be applicable to all. Below are some other more specific examples.

If a session was to be delivered to support the skills development of a group then the aim could be communicated with the statement "By the end of the session the participants will be able to *change gear smoothly and accurately*" This could be tested and the aim could be assessed as either met or not.

The group of 14 year olds on a residential outdoor course from school might be expected to develop their abilities to work together as a team. To assess the successful outcomes a review of the students' experiences would be appropriate.

A team of 16 year-olds undergoing Duke of Edinburgh Award training to use mountain bikes as part of their silver expedition need to develop their navigation skills prior to embarking on their venture. Using a route card and allowing them to lead sections would give an indication of ability and provide opportunity for navigation coaching.

Eight colleagues have come away for the weekend to the mountains to have an adventurous and exciting holiday on mountain bikes. To send them away better bikers, safe and covered in mud would be an appropriate outcome in this situation!

Although basic, each of the four statements above quickly demonstrates some of the wider aims of a mountain bike session and how a leader would employ different strategies to meet those aims and assess or evaluate their success. With a clear set of aims a leader becomes empowered and in control of their session with the ability to make clear and purposeful decisions.

'Failure to Plan means Planning to Fail'

3. TERRAIN

Planning where to take a group and what sort of terrain will be suitable depends on having prior knowledge of the other factors discussed in this section: aspirations, fitness, equipment and age. You will also have to consider logistics of transport, costs and other resources and accessibility of the area and facilities you are seeking to use. Plans should also reflect time of year and weather. For guidelines on terrain selection see **Terrain & Route Selection**.

4. ROUTE PLANNING

A detailed route plan allows any potential problems to be anticipated in advance, and should include escape routes in case of injury, bad weather or exhausted group members. Working out escape routes in advance performs two functions – you can work them out without stress, and it may help anyone who has to find you in an emergency. A route card should be small enough to be accessed easily but should not be relied on alone – always carry a map and compass.

The Appendix contains a sample route card. (see **Navigation** and **Emergency Planning** for further information on the use of route cards).

You can use a route card to work out distance, height, estimated time and to adjust plans if necessary according to ability, fitness and the prevailing conditions. Software can also help with planning, calculations such as distance and height gained, and route card production. See **Terrain & Route Selection** for some examples of mapping software which can be used to produce your own route cards.

A copy of your route plan should be left with somebody who knows what to do if you have not returned by a specified time. Don't forget to inform them of your safe return and retrieve the route plan in case somebody who doesn't know you're back safely finds it.

5. COMMUNICATION AND DECISION MAKING

The Teaching and Leadership section describes several leadership models which provide guidance on when the leader retains decision making (i.e. the leader takes all decisions), when to involve the group and to what extent the group will have decision making responsibility.

During the planning phase the leader should similarly decide on what stages, if any, can involve the group. The following stages should be included by the leader in the planning phase:

1. Collect information on the group, including age, sex, fitness, previous experience and the group's expectations for the session. (i.e. why do they want to do it)

2. Obtain parental consent forms for under 16 year olds, which should include details of any medical conditions, special needs and current medication being taken.

3. An emergency contact list should be prepared and a copy given to your base contact.

4. A detailed route should be prepared for the session taking into account the aspirations of the group, their ability and level of fitness

5. A risk assessment should be prepared for the session related to the group's abilities, weather conditions and time of year (see section on **Hazards & Risk Management**).

6. Equipment for the group (whether shared or personal) should be checked for safety, suitability and size/weight.

7. Meeting arrangements should be communicated to participants and parents/guardians, including, location, time and planned finishing time.

8. Information should be given to participants about what to bring including food and drink and what to carry it in.

9. The leader's repair kit and First Aid kit should be checked to ensure it's suitability for the session and that nothing is missing.

At the start of the session the leader should brief the group on the session and reach agreement on the objective of the session.

On return contact should be made with the base so that your late back procedures are not activated.

Finally, a good leader will review the session and note any lessons to be learned which could inform the planning and organisation of future sessions.

Communication aids

Mention has already been made of mobile phones elsewhere in this manual, including their use in communicating information in an emergency. A leader would be well advised to carry a mobile phone at all times, but it must be remembered that mobile phones can not be relied on in all areas, depending on the terrain and proximity to a transmitter.

2-way radios are an alternative option, although their range is relatively short, typically up to 3km. They are a popular means of staying in touch in the outdoors with skiers, climbers, event teams etc. Radios have the advantages of being fixed-cost (i.e. no call charge), and being generally reliable within their range of operation. Two or more radios can talk to each other, providing they are within range and using the same channel. With a bit of advance planning, a leader could arrange for radio communication to be available between the party and one or more bases within range of their location en route. Leaders of two or more groups within the same area could use radio communication to relay useful information about their group, navigation features, trail conditions, weather etc., allowing for a degree of remote teamwork.

Hazards & Risk Management

By the end of this section Leaders should be able to:-

- Understand the principles of risk assessment

- Know what the three levels of risk assessment are and when each is applied

- Describe the types of hazards encountered while mountain biking

- Explain how the interaction of hazards can increase the degree of risk to the group

- Carry out a risk assessment for a group ride

INTRODUCTION
In order to maximise the enjoyment of a mountain bike ride it needs to be challenging but safe. A well prepared leader and a motivated group should be able to experience excitement without danger, and adventure without hazard.

Some degree of risk is associated with all activities, including mountain biking. Assessing and managing identified hazards which could cause harm is the process described by **Risk Assessment**. In simple terms, it means looking at what could go wrong, and deciding how to prevent or minimise any problems occurring.

A leader in charge of a group needs to understand how to carry out a full risk assessment and how to modify a previous one. Although a leader's principle concern is the safety of the group, a risk assessment should also seek to minimise any risks to other outdoor users whom the group may comes into contact with.

THE PRINCIPLES OF RISK ASSESSMENT

- What are the hazards?

- Who might be affected by them?

- What safety measures need to be in place to reduce the risks to a reasonable level?

- Can the group leader ensure that the safety measures in place are adhered to?

- Can an assessment of the effectiveness of the safety measures and any proposed changes be made?

Carrying out a risk assessment is a relatively simple task once the basic principles outlined below are understood and applied to the context of a mountain bike ride.

1. Hazard – anything that could cause harm or injury

In the context of mountain biking a hazard could be physical, e.g. frozen ground, sharp rocks or fallen trees; mechanical – e.g. faulty brakes, a loose headset or worn tyres; or human – e.g. fatigue, inappropriate clothing or an existing injury or physical disability. Some hazards can be identified by checking out a route, pre-ride bike checks and monitoring the condition of group members before and during a ride. Other hazards can be predicted, for example through the use of weather forecasts.

2. Risk – the likelihood that someone will be harmed by a hazard

Once the hazards have been identified, they must be evaluated. How likely is it that the hazard will lead to an accident or harm to any group members ? What is the degree of risk for each hazard ? In the context of mountain biking, harm could occur to an individual directly through slipping or hitting an obstacle, or indirectly through faulty brakes or a sudden puncture resulting in a loss of control. Either way, not only is an individual hurt, but the ability of the group to continue will be affected.

3. Risk management – taking action to reduce the degree of risk

Any risks which are determined to be **high** must be considered significant and require action to be taken to reduce the risk to **low** or to an acceptable level. For example, the risk associated with extreme cold is high, somebody could easily get hypothermia, but can be reduced to low by taking account of weather conditions to avoid exposure and by ensuring adequate clothing is worn or carried and energy levels are maintained.

There will be a risk rating for every hazard, but it is also important to consider the interaction of two or more hazards which may be individually of low or medium risk, but collectively pose a medium or high risk. For example, a section of trail with slabs of rock may be low risk in the dry, but high risk when wet. The group factor must always be bourn in mind; even one ill-prepared rider or faulty bike in a group poses a risk to the entire group, and increases the chance of an accident or bad experience for everybody.

4. Review and appraise risk-controlling measures

Having carried out the risk assessment before an excursion, after the event you need to assess your control measures and comment on their effectiveness and record any changes which are required. A written risk assessment needs to be dated and signed with a reassessment date stated.

This last point leads us on to consider the **three levels of risk assessment**. These levels are progressive and the steps to carrying out a risk assessment (see below) would apply to each level.

1. **generic risk assessment**

2. **site-specific risk assessment**

3. **ongoing / dynamic risk assessment**

a) Generic Risk Assessment

As the name implies, a generic risk assessment concerns the general risks associated with the activity wherever and whenever it takes place. For mountain biking these would include safety of bikes and clothing. An example of generic risk-control measures would be bike safety checks and mandatory wearing of helmets.

Local authorities and some outdoor centres may have their own generic activity risk assessments, and would normally want to check any generic risk assessment prepared by an external individual or organisation. Centres licensed under the Adventure Activity Licensing Regulations 2004 should be considered safe in the leading, instructing and equipping of the activities stipulated on their licence, which may include mountain biking.

b) Site-specific Risk Assessment

Site-specific risk assessments will differ from place to place and group to group. They require more detailed knowledge about the hazards which may be specific to the location and to the individuals in the group.

Examples of location hazards include potentially dangerous sections of trail, river crossings, roads, electric fences etc. Hazards specific to the group could be medical conditions, behavioural problems or inexperience in mountain biking.

Physical hazards can be identified by a reconnaissance ride, which together with "local intelligence", can help to inform risk control measures. For example, local information can be obtained on the safest places to cross streams or roads, the timing of movements of farm animals, likelihood of sudden weather changes in the mountains, or ice affecting roads in frosty weather. Control measures for group specific hazards would include ensuring adequate supervision, having an agreed code of conduct and taking necessary precautions to deal with medical needs.

At this stage a leader should draw up a Plan B in case Plan A has become too hazardous, incorporating an alternative route and time schedule for the ride.

c) Ongoing / Dynamic Risk Assessment

While the first two levels of risk assessment are concerned with all hazards which can be indentified or reasonably predicted, and as such are pre-recorded, ongoing risk assessment is about making judgements and decisions to cope with changing levels of risk or unpredicted hazards. Examples would be worsening weather, injuries or illness, fatigue, inability to access a trail due to forestry operations or a road closure due to flooding or an accident. This is where Plan B may be come into use.

A leader must be able to assess the situation which is facing the group and make a decision based on best judgement and the knowledge he or she has about each individual, even if it means making the unpopular decision to end the ride in the interests of safety.

Emergency procedures (see this section) would come into play as the control measures for any emergency identified by ongoing risk assessment.

WHY CARRY OUT A RISK ASSESSMENT ?

It should be clear by understanding the principles of risk assessment what the leader's responsibilities are with respect to the safety of the group. However, carrying out a risk assessment can fulfill several purposes beyond legal and moral responsibility.

Carrying out a full risk assessment (from generic level to ongoing) can:

- Help prevent any accidents or emergencies occurring
- Avoid any expensive damage to bikes, clothing and equipment
- Help allay the concerns of anxious parents / teachers / care providers
- Increase the chances of all participants having a positive experience
- Indentify and increase knowledge of individual needs and differences in ability
- Give a leader greater confidence in his / her ability to supervise the group
- Improve a leader's leadership and group management skills
- Protect the reputation of the leader and of mountain biking as an activity
- Facilitate future group leading exercises

HOW TO CARRY OUT A RISK ASSESSMENT

The Management of Health & Safety at Work Regulations, from which risk assessment emanates, states that "a risk assessment should be suitable and sufficient, and ONLY THE SIGNIFICANT RISKS SHOULD BE RECORDED".

There are five steps to carrying out a risk assessment:

1. **Look** for the hazards
2. **Evaluate** the risks
3. **Record** the information
4. **Act** to reduce all risks to low
5. **Review** the risks

1. A site-specific risk assessment should be carried out in advance of every group ride. It is a good idea to do this with another leader or somebody who can help you record your findings.

The ideal time for a reconnaissance ride would be a week or two before your planned trip. If done too far in advance it is more likely that some features may have changed by the time you take your group out. On the other hand, if you do not leave sufficient time between your risk assessment and your group ride you may not have enough time to evaluate the risks and adjust your plans according to your assessment.

Pre-ride the route(s) you plan to use. Look for any physical hazards along the route – rocks, loose gravel, tree stumps, gates, steep slopes. Record any fixed features on a route map with symbols to identify the feature and notes explaining what the hazard is. Some hazards might not be apparent at the time of this initial assessment. Changes in weather can create new hazards, or change the nature of a hazard unexpectedly. A stream which you wish to cross may become a small torrent after heavy rain, for example. A road or track may be safe without traffic, but at certain times of the day or at a weekend it might become busy and possibly dangerous. So try to think about how changing conditions could change the nature of the hazards  you encounter. Seek local knowledge or information sources on factors such as weather, deer stalking, visitor usage etc. Find out if there are any other events taking place on the same day as your planned trip, such as other sporting events, a country fair, a public rally etc, which would make it safer for you to change the time or date of your of your ride.

2. Think about each hazard you have identified How might it cause harm to your group, who is most likely to be harmed, and what is the degree of risk ? When doing this you have to try and anticipate how the risk rating might change in different conditions, as outlined above. You may have a parallel risk rating for each hazard in dry and wet weather conditions, for example.

By this stage you should have built up a picture of what and where the significant hazards are and identified the risks which will need to be controlled. You also need to consider the group you are leading (refer to the above sections on "The Group" and "Leadership") – factors such as group size, experience, equipment, fitness and skill levels will affect the rating of any risks you will have to manage.

The table below gives examples of hazards in the three main categories and the types of action which may be taken to reduce the associated risks. This list is by no means exhaustive, and a leader should expect to identify other hazards, depending on their environment.

Examples of hazards and risk controlling measures

Hazard	What could happen and to whom	Risk controlling measures
Physical Steep descents Gravel / loose rock Wet rocks Drop-offs Tree stumps & roots Overhanging / side branches Boggy ground / mud Large puddles Streams Ice Bad weather Low light Roads Horses Dogs Farm animals Walkers Other mountain bikers	All members of the group Other trail users Injury (minor) Injury (severe) Damage to bikes Hypothermia Navigation problems Separation of group Fatigue Conflict with other users	Skills training Pre-ride briefing Bike safety checks Adequate clothing worn / carried Helmets – obligatory Adequate tools & repair kit First aid kit and training Bike lights fitted / carried Group management – (hazard warnings, instructions to dismount, reduce speed etc) Route maps Navigation skills & aids Off-road Code of Conduct Alternative route(s) plan Emergency procedures in place
Human Inexperience Lack of fitness Lack of skills Existing injuries Low energy Fatigue Low morale Lack of confidence Physical disabilities Medical conditions Social problems (drugs, alcohol) Bad behaviour	All members of the group Other trail users Injury / re-injury Medical emergency Loss of control Separation of group Conflict within group	Prior group knowledge Appropriate terrain / route choice Medication carried Group warm up Agreed communication shouts / signals Code of conduct Group management Additional supervision First aid kit and training Motivational techniques Good navigation Alternative route(s) plan Emergency procedures in place

3. Record your findings using a risk assessment form. The Appendix contains a sample **Risk Assessment Form** which could be used, or adapted to suit. The **Bike Safety Checklist**, also in the Appendix, could be used as a part of an equipment risk assessment. You can return to this form if the risks change and your assessment needs to be modified. Your employer, insurance provider, a site owner or others involved with your group may wish to see a copy of your completed risk assessment.

4. Minimise the risks Now you have gathered your information and evaluated the risks, what can you do to minimise the risks and prevent harm occurring to any of your group ? What type of action you might take will depend on the nature of the hazard, and to a certain extent, when it is encountered.

Hazards identified in advance of a ride must be reduced or eliminated at this stage. For example, any mechanical problems with the group's bikes need to be attended to immediately. Anyone who does not have a helmet and appropriate clothing will need to acquire some, or be able to borrow from others who have spares. These basic safety points should be part of the **generic risk assessment** and should be routinely addressed before every outing.

If you have identified potentially dangerous sections of trail on your reconnaissance ride you need to decide what actions will be necessary to reduce the risk of anyone coming to harm here. Control measures will include briefing the group about these hazards and issuing instructions such as "dismount" or "slow down" well in advance.

A leader needs to know how to practice good **group management** in this respect. Your position within a moving group is going to be important in preventing any accidents due to riders getting too far ahead or losing control. Being at the front of the group can be useful for slowing the group down before a steep descent or tricky section, controlling the pace of over enthusiastic riders, navigating, and showing a good line to take on single track. Leading from the rear of a group may be best when the group is tiring or when individual members need encouragement.

5. Review the risks A crucial stage of risk assessment is reviewing the risks. Even the best risk assessments involve a degree of prediction and informed guess-work. The environment and the human condition are dynamic, not static, and unanticipated changes can occur. In particular, you need to monitor the condition of the group and continually assess their safety by observation, communication and asking questions about their well-being. How are the group's energy levels, morale and comfort ? Is the weather taking a turn for the worse ? Have the riding conditions been harder than expected ? As a leader, you will have to think on your feet (or on your pedals!) and make decisions to prevent risk levels from increasing due to changes in the factors you are monitoring. This is the process of **ongoing / dynamic risk assessment** (see above).

After a ride, review your risk assessment and your risk control strategy. Make notes and try to use your experience, positive and negative, to help you with future planning and risk management. Record your findings using a risk assessment form

TCL v MBL considerations

Leaders should be fully aware of the criteria of a Trail Cycle Leader and Mountain Bike Leader (see **Introduction**) which define their respective operating environments. These criteria have been devised against a risk management background to place safe and realistic limits on where and when (time of day and season) groups can be led.

A group operating in more remote and technically difficult MBL terrain is potentially exposed to higher risks, than a group in TCL terrain. These risks must be controlled by matching the experience, abilities, motivation and equipment of your group to the terrain and routes you choose. This is a critical part of controlling the risks when planning any ride.

Legal Issues & Liability

By the end of this section Leaders should:-

- Understand their principal responsibilities with respect to good practice and child protection

- Know where to obtain further information and help

- Understand the implications of insurance, duty of care and parental consent for safe and legal leadership practice

- Be clear about the operating conditions of TCL and MBL awards in relation to competencies defined by Adventure Activities Licensing Authority suitable for leading groups off-road

INTRODUCTION

Leaders, being in a position of responsibility, must have an awareness of their moral and legal responsibilities to others who may be affected by their actions. This is as much about setting personal and professional standards of good practice as it is about simply fulfilling legal requirements. Therefore, a leader who wishes to take pride in his or her work and to set a good example of leadership should be willing to accept and embrace their legal responsibilities for their own protection, and the protection of those whom they are leading. This section outlines the main issues which a Leader must have an awareness of and how this understanding should inform Trail Cycle and Mountain Bike Leadership practices. Some of these issues are large topics in their own right and can not be covered in detail within this manual, however references are given which provide further sources of information.

LEADER INSURANCE

All Leaders should have some form of insurance cover for their own protection. Membership of Scottish Cycling/British Cycling (see **Introduction**) at Silver or Gold level provides entitlement to Third Party (Public Liability) insurance, free legal advice and assistance for members resident in the UK. Entitlement to Professional Indemnity insurance for registered British Cycling Coaches and Leaders who are Silver or Gold members is dependent on evidence of Leaders having attended both First Aid and Child Protection training. To gain automatic entitlement to Professional Indemnity insurance, Trail Cycle Leaders should submit evidence of Child Protection training to Scottish Cycling at the time of membership application.

Leaders who are working for a Local Authority, outdoor centre, or some other organisation may be covered by their employer's insurance policy. It is important to check this and to check the details of the policy so that all conditions are met.

It is the responsibility of every Leader to check the details of the insurance policy (or that of their employer) under which they are operating, and abide by the conditions, adjusting practice and factors such as group size where necessary.

DUTY OF CARE

"Duty of Care" refers to the responsibility of a leader to look after a child (or a dependent adult) in their charge. It is often used in conjunction with the phrase "in loco parentis", meaning in place of the child's parent or guardian. A person "in loco parentis" stands in the place of a parent and owes a duty of care to the child equal to the duty of care owed by a reasonable parent, that is a careful parent. The careful parent will avoid activities and situations likely to cause harm to a child in his or her care. This duty requires careful thinking ahead and planning.

Scottish Cycling's Code of Conduct contains guidance on how to act responsibly in a position of care by adopting high personal and professional standards.

CHILD PROTECTION & GOOD PRACTICE

One of the most important legal issues which Leaders must be informed about is Child Protection. Leaders have a legal and ethical responsibility, firstly to protect children they may come into contact with from abuse, and secondly, themselves from wrongful accusations.

Mountain biking is just like any other sport or outdoor activity in providing many opportunities for abuse and bad practice to occur. Leaders must be aware of this potential in planning and assessing their own leadership practices. They must also be able to recognize the signs of potential child abuse and take appropriate action when a child discloses information to them, or when there is suspicion of abuse or evidence of bad practice by a colleague or another adult known to the Leader.

Anybody working with children or vulnerable adults has an important role to play in ensuring good practice is adhered to and in helping to identify and put a stop to child abuse.

CHILD PROTECTION AND GOOD PRACTICE TRAINING

It is beyond the scope of this manual to give more than an introduction to the issue of Child Protection. However, the SMBLA strongly recommends that all Leaders undertake Child Protection training by attending an approved course provided by an employer or organisations such as **sport**scotland or NSPCC (see Useful Contacts for details of these course providers). Leaders are expected to operate within the guidelines of Scottish Cycling's **Child Protection Policy** and **Code of Conduct**, or that of your employer under whose authority you are working.

SCOTTISH CYCLING CHILD PROTECTION POLICY

The full Scottish Cycling **Child & Vulnerable Adult Protection Policy** is available to Leaders on request or from the Scottish Cycling website www.scottishcycling.com. All Leaders should familiarize themselves with the Policy and know their responsibilities with respect to protection of participants and themselves.

The three key responsibilities are summarized below. All these issues should be covered in more detail in an approved Child Protection training course.

1. Be able to recognise the signs and indicators of child abuse

There are four main kinds of child abuse: physical, emotional, sexual, or neglect. Abused children may display a variety of behaviours; they may be aggressive or withdrawn, they may be nervous and are often reluctant to take part in group activities. Physical signs of injury or neglect may or may not be apparent; a child will often try to hide these. Bear in mind that children can show disturbed behaviour or have bumps and bruises for any number of reasons and these signs do not necessarily indicate abuse. Children's behaviour must be viewed within the context of their social background and other activities they are involved in. However, such signs should give you grounds for concern, especially if the child is reluctant to talk to you when questioned about the underlying causes. If a child whom you work with regularly repeatedly shows one or more of the possible indicators of abuse then there may be grounds for concern over their safety and well-being.

2. Follow the policy and procedures of Scottish Cycling or your organisation for dealing with suspected child abuse

An abused child or vulnerable adult is <u>not</u> your sole responsibility. However, you can take steps to inform others about your concerns so that appropriate actions can be taken. Your organisation should have a designated Child Protection officer whom you can speak to in confidence. They will advise on whether to involve parents or guardians or social services. Only where a child requires urgent medical attention should the situation be treated as an emergency.

3. Reduce the risk to yourself of potential accusations of child abuse and promote good practice in working with children

As child abuse is a highly emotive issue and public awareness is being raised in trying to tackle the problem, anyone working with children is at risk of being falsely accused of abuse. To protect yourself from this risk you must adopt good practice and implement a plan to follow procedure.

GOOD PRACTICE FOR WORKING WITH CHILDREN

The following advice is reproduced from Scottish Cycling's **Code of Conduct** for the Protection of Children & Vulnerable Adults:

- Make sport fun, enjoyable and promote fair play.
- Always work in an open environment e.g. avoid private / unobserved situations and encourage an open environment for activities.
- Treat all children and vulnerable adults equally, with respect and dignity.
- Put the welfare of each child or vulnerable adult first before winning or achieving performance goals.
- Give enthusiastic and constructive feedback rather than negative criticism.
- Ensure that if any form of manual or physical support is required for a child or vulnerable adult, it is provided openly, the child or vulnerable adult is informed of what is being done and their consent is obtained.
- Deliver educational instruction first verbally; secondly role-modelled; and thirdly, and only if necessary, with hands on which must be accompanied by telling the child or vulnerable adult where you are putting your hands, why it is necessary and obtaining their consent.
- Involve parents, guardians and carers wherever possible.
- Build balanced relationships based on mutual trust that empower children and vulnerable adults to share in the decision making process.
- Recognise the developmental needs and capacity of children and vulnerable adults, avoid excessive training or competition and either pushing them against their will or putting undue pressure on them

In addition to the above Code, the following guidelines for working with groups of children should be applied:

- Avoid situations where you are the sole adult in the company of a child
- Always obtain parental consent for minors (see below)
- Address all safety issues through a full risk assessment (see Hazards & Risk Management)
- Meet the physical needs of children in your care for food, water, warmth and rest
- Ensure all adults who may be assisting you with supervision adopt the same practices

The **Child Protection Checklist** in the Appendix can be used to record useful information for you to have readily available when working with children. Finding out this information in advance will allow you to act more quickly and confidently should the need arise.

VETTING SUITABILITY – DISCLOSURE SCOTLAND CHECKS
In addition to Child Protection training, leaders working with children may be required by law to have an **Enhanced Disclosure Check**. The Disclosure service is provide by the Criminal Records Bureau (CRB) to employers and voluntary organisations to enable them to check records which may make an individual unsuitable for working with children. Any adult who is in substantial and regular contact with children should be subject to an Enhanced Disclosure Check before working with children.

There are some circumstances in which a local authority or staff in charge may decide that a Disclosure Check is not necessary. An example would be a one-off or short-term involvement by an individual with a group of children in an activity, where the group continues to be supervised at all times by a member of staff who is Disclosure Checked and trained in child protection. In other circumstances a Disclosure check will be judged essential, such as a residential excursion, or leading a group of children with special needs. Any TCL or MBL should seek the advice of the organisation they intend to work with well in advance, as Disclosure checks take several weeks to process. Disclosure checks can be provided by Scottish Cycling for leaders carrying out work on SC's behalf.

Further advice can be gained from Disclosure Scotland, www.disclosurescotland.co.uk.

PARENTAL CONSENT
Parental consent must be sought for any activity or outing planned for under 16 year olds (in Scotland). A leader will be acting "in loco parentis" (as a parent) for any young person defined as a "minor" in law.

A consent form will clearly outline your planned activities, start and end time, location and inherent risks. The consent form is your "contract of agreement" with a parent or guardian, so it must give sufficient detail

about what is planned, and you must not stray outside of this plan once it is agreed to.

There is a sample **Parental Consent Form** in the Appendix with the basic information which must be provided. Your employer may issue a standard form for you use, but you should provide supporting information for parents so that they are fully informed of what they are agreeing (or not) that their child is involved in. Providing comprehensive information to parents will help to reassure them, give you confidence that you have their support for your activities and leave you less open to any claims of negligence.

ADVENTURE ACTIVITIES LICENSING

The Adventure Activities Licensing Authority (AALA) is the body responsible for inspecting adventure activity providers and Local Authorities whose provision falls within the scope of the Act, on behalf of the Department of Education and Skills (DfES). Providers which meet the appropriate standards of good practice will be issued with a licence for these activities by the Licensing Authority. Most Local Authorities recognise this official approval and consider AALA-licensed centres safe in the leading and equipping of activities on their license.

Mountain biking is an AALA licensable activity, coming under the category of "Trekking", which includes trekking on foot, on horse, on skis and on a bike. AALA licensable trekking activities are those which take place **above 600m and / or more than 30 minutes walk (or 2.5 km whichever is nearer) from an accessible road or refuge**. The Mountain Bike Leader qualification was prepared to operate in the scope of adventure activity licensing. The Trail Cycle Leader was designed to operate outwith licensing terrain. (see **Introduction** and the table over the page).

WHO REQUIRES A LICENCE?

According to the Adventure Activities Licensing Regulations which came into effect on 1st April 1996 (since reviewed and ammended 9th June 2004) persons are required to hold a licence if that person:

Provides facilities for certain adventure activities to young people under 18 years of age in return for payment

or

Is a local authority, and the facilities are provided to an educational establishment in respect of the pupils of such an establishment

(The full Statutory Instruments relating to this legislation, and further guidance on mountain biking, are available on the Adventure Activities Licensing Authority website www.aala.org.uk)

WHAT LEVEL OF COMPETENCE IS REQUIRED TO LEAD ACTIVITIES WHICH ARE LICENSABLE?

The table on the following page shows the competence of SMBLA qualifications which AALA recognises as suitable to lead groups under defined conditions and terrain. MBL and TCL, while not exclusively recognised by AALA as qualifications in mountain bike leadership, are the only national governing body (NGB) awards. Local authorities or other organisations would generally seek an NGB qualification as a measure of competence for leaders of activities which are licensable. Scottish Cycling and British Cycling are listed NGBs in the Scottish Executive's *Health and Safety on Educational Excursions: A Good Practice Guide* (Annex B) (available at www.scotland.gov.uk). The SMBLA awards are also "stand alone", in that they are recognized by AALA as providing competence (in all but winter conditions) without the need for an additional on-foot qualification.

It should be noted that with respect to assessing competence to lead licensable activities, a local authority, school or other organisation may seek, in addition to paper qualification(s) (TCL/MBL certificate, first aid qualification, SC/BC membership), references, verification of personal skills and relevant experience.

SMBLA Tutors, recognised as "Technical Advisors" for AALA on mountain biking, may be nominated to perform the following services by a facilities provider:

- o clarify areas of uncertainty which neither the provider nor the instructors involved are suitably knowledgeable, experienced or qualified to address, e.g. advise on particular venues and or equipment to be used; conditions prevailing; required competence levels for given circumstances
- o Ratify the competence of their non-NGB qualified staff or conduct staff training
- o be consulted on any issues identified by AALA inspection, and contained in a report issued to the provider

OFF-ROAD CYCLING TECHNICAL COMPETENCE QUALIFICATION MATRIX

(adapted from Adventure Activities Licensing Authority Ref: C/Int 47v07 6.1.2 Off-Road Cycling: Leader Qualifications, Recognised Awards and Training and Assessment Safety Criteria)

Operating Environment	Leader Competence	Technical Advisor
Mountain Country – Winter Conditions	Mountain Bike Leader *plus* the relevant on-foot qualification (i.e. Mountain Leader Winter)	SMBLA Tutor *plus* the relevant mountaineering qualification (i.e. Mountaineering Instructor)
Mountain Country – Intermediate Conditions some snow (e.g. a light dusting or avoidable patches or lightly freezing conditions (e.g. an overnight frost) prevalent or forecast	Mountain Bike Leader	SMBLA Tutor *plus* the relevant mountaineering qualification (i.e. Mountaineering Instructor)
Mountain Country – Summer Conditions	Mountain Bike Leader	SMBLA Tutor
Lowland Country – Off-road Cycling Cycleways, tracks or other technical routes in open country more than a 30 minute walk (or 2.5 km whichever is less) from a refuge or accessible road	Mountain Bike Leader	SMBLA Tutor
Lowland Country – trail riding (non-licensable) Public highways, cycleways, forestry tracks and non-technical routes no further than a 30 minute walk (or 2.5 km whichever is less) from a refuge or accessible road	Trail Cycle Leader (or Mountain Bike Leader)	SMBLA Tutor

Mountain Biking in Scotland

Whether you want technical singletrack, relaxed scenic routes, North Shore style constructions or a wilderness expedition you will find it all in Scotland. The International Mountain Bicycling Association (IMBA) has just rated Scotland as one of the top five destinations in the world for mountain biking, and the best outside North America. Scotland was also voted number one in the world for mountain biking under the 'People's Choice" category in an on-line poll.

As well as a growing number of purpose-built and regularly maintained trails, many of which have on-site facilities such as cafés, bike washes and showers, there are also miles and miles of natural trails which were used by cyclists long before mountain biking became a sport. Scotland has a long history of off-road cycling and the bicycle has always been a popular way for walkers and climbers to reach more remote areas. Many long distance walks such as the Great Glen Way can be biked and there are a couple of Scottish off-road coast to coast routes too.

The trails which are now being developed across the country mean that mountain biking is becoming more accessible, with way-marked and graded all-weather trails offering something for everyone from the complete novice to expert riders. The Forestry Commission have been instrumental in developing many of these trails, including the hugely successful 7 Stanes in the Scottish Borders and the new trails at Laggan in the Highlands. They are currently working in conjunction with other organisations to create a consistent trail grading system throughout the country.

There are downhill courses at Innerleithen, Ae and Fort William, all of which offer transport to the top. The Nevis Range ski area and Leanachan Forest, Fort William, have hosted rounds of the UCI Mountain Bike World Cup since 2002, and in 2007 will host the UCI Mountain Bike and Trials World Championships. The World Cup downhill, 4-X and cross country courses at Fort William are open to ride all year round.

There are new trails in Lochgilphead, Drumlanrig Castle, Pollock Park near Glasgow, the Black Isle, and at Fochabers in Morayshire. Trail builders in the Carron Valley, near Stirling, have managed to raise £30,000 through a number of community based funds to aid their efforts.

As a side attraction, Drumlanrig Castle has a Cycle Museum containing a replica of the "velocipede", the first pedal cycle invented by local blacksmith, Kirkpatrick Macmillan in 1840.

Scottish Local Authorities are currently identifying "Core Path Networks", and all have appointed Access Officers with this responsibility. Core Paths are principally local paths which form a network of local access for multiple user categories, including cycling. As paths are formally identified, issues of signage and maintenance will be addressed, so improving information and access to many existing paths for cyclists. See the **Access** section for related information.

Further information on many of the places mentioned above can be found under "Places to ride" in the **Useful Contacts** section. Leaflets are available for Forestry Commission routes, and there are various books and maps available from book shops and bike shops. Local bike shops are usually the best source of information on where to ride, and most of them are happy to help.

Mountain Biking as a Sport

INTRODUCTION

Riding bikes off road and away from the inherent risks and conflicts with traffic is an excellent opportunity for a broad cross-section of society to become involved in the sport of cycling, and for them to engage with the outdoors in an exciting and accessible way. It promotes the use of urban as well as remote environments, and allows the benefits of an 'outdoor activity' to transfer into the everyday lives of participants. Mountain biking can be a spiritual and enjoyable experience and it is quick to reward those who desire to improve their skills by regular riding. For many it has become their first-choice sport and a pathway to elite fitness and competition.

Of all the cyclesport disciplines, mountain biking is by far the most popular in Scotland, with events in the Scottish Race Calendar regularly attracting several hundred riders of all ages and abilities. It is a very spectator-friendly sport and some of the race venues are within areas of high scenic value. Scotland is acknowledged as hosting some of the best mountain bike racing in the UK, with many competitors traveling from south of the Border to access more challenging and technical courses.

This section aims to provide an introduction to the sport of mountain biking in its various forms and provide some guidance on how to get involved. The complimentary section, "Mountain Biking in Scotland" gives ideas on where to ride and some of the highlights of mountain biking in Scotland.

SUB-DISCIPLINES OF MOUNTAIN BIKING

Mountain Biking is undoubtedly a sport for everyone, whatever their age or ability. The two main branches of competitive mountain biking, cross-country and downhill, are intersected by a growing area of participation events which include trailquest (mountain bike orienteering) and single-day and multi-day endurance events.

Downhill, with its thrills and spills, is fast becoming the most popular discipline in the sport of mountain biking. Competitors race on full suspension bikes and wear full-face helmets and body armour to protect against the dangers of a high speed crash. Both power and speed are needed to cover the ground as fast as possible, and exceptional bike handling skills, honed through hours and hours of practice. At the top level, downhill requires a high level of fitness, but anyone with some experience of mountain biking can have a go and test themselves against the course.

Cross-country racing has more of an endurance element than downhill, but the technical nature of some courses requires a high degree of skill as well. Within cross-country and downhill events there are races for all categories of rider, from Juvenile to Grand Veteran. The Fun category is where many first-time racers start and the Fun race is the ideal entry-level event.

The sister discipline to cross-country is **cyclo-cross**. Cyclo-cross races take place on a short off-road circuit and generally last about an hour, considerably shorter than the average cross-country race which lasts 2-3 hours. You can use a mountain bike for cyclo-cross races in Scotland, but not for cyclo-cross events in the British series. The dedicated cyclo-cross bike is more like a road bike, but with wider knobbly tires, cantilever or V-brakes and a frame which allows greater mud clearance. It will be lighter than a mountain bike (at least one with full suspension), which makes it easier to carry on sections of the course where it may be faster to dismount and run with your bike. However, because cyclo-cross is a winter sport and ground conditions tend to be muddy, using a mountain bike is often no disadvantage.

The sport of mountain bike orienteering, known as **trailquest**, is growing in popularity. Trailquest is an activity which requires many of the skills developed by mountain bike Leader training: navigation, route choice, core skills, planning and group organisation. A typical trailquest event consists of 20-30 control sites positioned alongside tracks and trails which competitors must identify on pre-printed maps, or by copying from master maps onto their own Ordnance Survey Map or from grid references. Depending on the event, between 2 and 7 hours are allowed to visit as many sites as possible in order to score the highest possible points total. The majority of trailquest events are held south of the Border; for a full list and more details of how to enter visit www.trailquest.co.uk

There are several well established **endurance** or ultra-endurance mountain bike events in the UK and abroad. These events are usually supported by one or more major sponsors and are often more like a mini festival than a one day race. Sleepless in the Saddle, held annually near Stoke-on-Trent is one of the most popular 24 hour endurance events in Britain, attracting several hundred individual and team entries (www.sleeplessinthesaddle.com). If you don't fancy riding all day and night, but still want a challenge you could choose to ride one of the MTB Marathon Series (www.mtb-marathon.co.uk) organised in various locations around the country.

For anyone who considers themselves a strong endurance rider, the TransAlp is the ultimate test. Ridden over eight days, three countries, 570km and 19,000m of climbing, the TransAlp is not for the faint hearted, but to sweeten the bitter pill of pain there is the pleasure of being in some of the most spectacular mountain terrain in Europe. The Grand Raid Cristalp is a similarly tough Alpine marathon, held in the Swiss Alps over nine days. These events attract both pros and serious amateurs, numbering several thousand in total, and are truly international in their membership.

HOW TO GET INVOLVED IN RACING

In Scotland mountain bike races are organised by the Scottish Cross-country Association (SXC), and the Scottish Downhill Association (SDA), on behalf of Scottish Cycling. The British XC and DH series are organised by British Cycling (www.britishcycling.org.uk). The Scottish Race Calendar consists of a series of seven XC and DH events, and Scottish Championships in each discipline. Both the series and championship events attract large numbers of people – riders, supporters and spectators, especially in downhill, and make a great day out in the country.

There are no pre-requirements to ride in Scottish Cycling mountain bike events, other than a bike and a helmet, but in order to be eligible for the Scottish Championship you must be both a Scottish Cycling member and a member of a Scottish Club. Race dates and entry forms can be obtained from the SXC and SDA websites:

Scottish Cross-Country Association www.sxc.org.uk
Scottish Downhill Association www.sda-races.com

Joining a club which caters for mountain biking or a dedicated mountain bike club is a good way to access mountain bike sport and meet other riders whom you can learn from, ride with and share transport to events. There are details of Scottish cycling clubs on the Scottish Cycling website (www.scottishcycling.com) and in the Scottish Cycling Handbook which is published annually.

Bibliography

 The texts below are additional reading matter which the mountain biker and mountain bike leader may find useful to increase their knowledge of the topics covered in this manual and to have as guides and reference books.

NAVIGATION

Advanced Mountain Biking, Derek Purdy, 1995 ppb., A & C Black, ISBN 185688046X.
Includes sections on bike choice and preparation, map reading, weather forecasting and mountain rescue.

Mountaincraft and Leadership, Eric Langmuir, 1995, Scottish Sports Council – sportscotland, ISBN 1850602956.

Land Navigation, Wally Keay, 1994, Ordnance Survey, ISBN 0319008452.
Explains the basics of navigation from grid references to complex navigation in remote highland/mountain areas.

Map and Compass: The Art of Navigation, Peter Hawkins, 2004, Cicerone Press, ISBN 1852843942.
Using plenty of diagrams, OS and Harvey Maps to illustrate points in the text, this book takes you logically through the various stages of learning map and compass skills. Includes a look at GPS systems and mapping software.

CORE SKILLS

Mountain Bike Like a Champion: Master the Techniques to Tackle the Toughest Terrain, Ned Overend & Ed Pavelka, 1999, Rodale Press, ISBN 1579540813.
Top tips from mountain bike ace, Ned Overend whose experience and skill drills inspire and explain how to become a better rider.

Mountain Bike!: A Manual of Beginning to Advanced Technique, William Nealy, 1992, Menasha Ridge Press, ISBN: 0897321146

Mountain Biking Skills, Strickland et al, 1996, Rodale Press ISBN 0875963005.
A book aimed at the "improver", full of tips, humour and inspiration.

Ultimate Guide to Mountain Biking, Steve Geal & Ronbin Kitchin, 2001, HarperCollinsWillow, ISBN: 0007110871.
With authoritative content, this book is for all mountain bikers, from the relative beginner to the experienced practitioner, offering practical advice and tips on how to improve your skills

ACCESS

The Scottish Glens, P.D. Koch-Osborne Cicerone Press 1. The Cairngorm Glens 2. The Atholl Glens 3. The Glens of Rannoch 4. The Trossachs Glens 5. Argyll Glens 6. The Great Glen 7. The Angus Glens 8. Knoydart to Morvern 9. The Glens of Ross-shire
A series of guides for mountain bikers and walkers, with hand drawn maps giving a good deal of detail.

Mountain Bike Guide: Inverness, the Great Glen and the Cairngorms, Timothy King and Derek Purdy, 2004, The Ernest Press, ISBN 0948153733.
One of a series of 17 route guides covering much of the UK (this is currently the only Scottish title).

Exploring Scottish Hill Tracks: For Walkers and Mountain Bikers, Ralph Storer, 1994, David & Charles, ISBN 0715302574.
Describes a selection of routes in the Scottish Highlands and Islands.

Scottish Hill Tracks, Moir, Bennet & Stone 1999, Scottish Rights of Way and Access Society, ISBN 0950281182.
A great aid to route planning where the requirement is to link a series of routes cross-country, covering roads, tracks and paths, some of them remote. Accompanied by a useful (removable) map.

TRAILSIDE REPAIRS

The Bike Book, Fred Milson (ed.), 2003, Haynes Group, ISBN 1844250008.
Well illustrated "how-to" guide, covering the most popular range of bikes and components in detail.

Mountain Bike Owners Manual, Lennard Zinn, 1998, VeloPress, ISBN 1884737471.
A clear and fun maintenance manual, explaining the workings of parts as well as how to effect repairs.

Mountain Bike Performance Handbook, Lennard Zinn, 1998, Bicycle Books Inc., ISBN 0933201958

Zinn and the Art of Mountain Bike Maintenance, Lennard Zinn, 2001, VeloPress, ISBN 1884737994.
Useful guide to mountain bike maintenance, illustrating tools, components and a wide range of repairs.

Mountain Bike Maintenance: The Illustrated Manual, Melanie Allwood, 2004, Firefly Books Ltd, ISBN 155297734X.
A very practical guide to mountain bike maintenance.

Mountain Bike Maintenance and Repair, Paul Vincent, 2002, Hamlyn, ISBN 0600607798, 2002.

Mountain Bike Maintenance and Repair, Thomas Roegner, 2003, Van der Plas Publications, ISBN 1892495376.

EXPEDITION PLANNING

The Backpacker's Cookbook, David Coustic, 1996, Neil Wilson Publishing Ltd, ISBN 1897784384.
An inspired guide to camp cooking, describing a range of simple but tasty one-pot meals made from real food, with tips on stoves and cooking equipment.

Expedition Guide, Wally Keay, 1995, Duke of Edinburgh Award Scheme, ISBN 0905425146

How to Shit in the Woods: An Environmentally Sound Approach to a Lost Art, Kathleen Meyer, 1994, Ten Speed Press, ISBN 0898156270.
A frank and practical guide to a vital part of expeditioning.

FUEL & HYDRATION

Sport Nutrition, Jeukendrup, A.E. & Gleson, M., 2004, Human Kinetics Europe Ltd, ISBN 0736034048.

WEATHER

Mountain Weather: A Practical Guide for Hillwalkers and Climbers in the British Isles, David Pedgley 2004, Cicerone Press, ISBN 1852842563.

The Weather Handbook, Alan Watts, 2004, Adlard Coles Nautical, ISBN 0713669381.
This book explains how to combine information given in weather forecasts with the reader's own observations to arrive at a correct assessment of what the coming weather is likely to be.

LEADERSHIP

Leading & Managing Groups in the Outdoors, K. Ogilvie, 1993, NAOI Publications, ISBN: 1898555001

Teaching Physical Education, M. Mosston & S. Ashworth, 2002, Allyn & Bacon, ISBN 0205340938.
"Offers teachers/leaders a foundation for understanding the decision-making structures that exist in all teaching/learning environments, and for recognising the variables that increase effectiveness while teaching physical education."

GENERAL

Mountain Bike Fitness Training, John Metcalfe, 2004, Mainstream Publishing, ISBN 1840188588.
Includes detailed descriptions of do-it-yourself fitness tests, skill drills and training exercises designed to improve off-road fitness. Although focused on cross-country and downhill racing, other chapters deal with expeditions and endurance mountain biking.

Hill Walking: The Official Handbook of the Mountain Leader and Walking Group Leader Schemes, Steve Long, 2003, The Mountain Training Trust, ISBN 0954151100.
Valuable reference book covering navigation, weather and related topics from a hill walking leadership perspective.

Useful Contacts

GENERAL

Adventure Activities Licensing Authority
17 Lambourne Crescent
Cardiff Business Park
Llanishen
Cardiff
CF14 5GF
Tel. 029 2075 5715
www.aala.org.uk

British Cycling
National Cycling Centre
Stuart Street
Manchester
M11 4DQ
Tel. 0161 274 2010
www.britishcycling.org.uk

Child Protection in Sport
CHILDREN 1ST
Sussex House
61 Sussex Street
Kinning Park
Glasgow
G41 1DY
Tel. 0141 418 5674
cpinsport@children1st.org.uk
www.children1st.org.uk

CTC (Cyclists Touring & Campaigning)
69 Meadrow, Godalming
Surrey
GU7 3HS
Tel. 0870 873 0060
cycling@ctc.org.uk
www.ctc.org.uk

CTC Scotland
www.ctcscotland.org.uk

CTC Cymru
www.ctc-wales.org.uk

Cycling Scotland
The Pentagon Suite
Washington Street
Glasgow
www.cyclingscotland.org

Disclosure Scotland
PO Box 250
Glasgow
G51 1YU
Tel. 0870 609 6006
info@disclosurescotland.co.uk
www.disclosurescotland.co.uk

Fort William World Cup
Rare Management
17 Calton Road
Edinburgh
EH8 8DL
Tel. 0131 557 3012
mtb@raremanagement.co.uk
www.fortwilliamworldcup.co.uk

Glenmore Lodge
Aviemore
Inverness-shire
PH22 1QU
Tel. 01479 861 256
www.glenmorelodge.org.uk

International Mountain Bicycling Association UK (IMBA-UK)
www.imba-uk.com

Institute for Outdoor Learning
The Barn
Plumpton Old Hall
Plumpton
Penrith
CA11 9NP
01768 885800
institute@outdoor-learning.org
www.outdoor-learning.org

Mountain Bothies Association
enquiries@mountainbothies.org.uk
www.mountainbothies.org.uk

**Mountain Leader Training –
Scotland**
Glenmore
Aviemore
PH22 1QU
Tel. 01479 861 248
www.mltuk.org

**Mountain Leader Training –
England**
MLTE Registered Office
Development Officer
177-179 Burton Road
Manchester
M20 2BB
Tel. 08700 104878
www.mlte.org

**Mountain Leader Training –
Northern Ireland**
Tollymore M.C.
Bryansford
Newcastle
BT 2BB
Tel. 02843 722 158
admin@tollymoremc.com

Mountain Leader Training – Wales
Capel Curig
Conway
LL24 0ET
Tel. 01690 720248
www.mltw.org

**The Mountaineering Council of
Scotland**
The Old Granary
West Mill Street
Perth
PH1 5QP
Tel. 01738 638227
info@mountaineering-
scotland.org.uk
www.mountaineering-scotland.org.uk

NSPCC Child Protection Training
NSPCC National Training Centre
3 Gilmour Close
Beaumont Leys
Leicester

LE4 1EZ
Tel. 0116 234 7225
www.nspcc.org.uk/inform/training

Paths for All Partnership
Inglewood House
Tullibody Road
ALLOA FK10 2HU
Tel. 01259 218888
info@pathsforall.org.uk
www.pathsforall.org.uk

**Scottish Advisory Panel for
Outdoor Education (SAPOE)**
www.sapoe.ik.org

**Scottish Cross-Country
Association (SXC)**
Tel. 01560 600 805
info@sxc.org.uk
www.sxc.org.uk

Scottish Downhill Association
sda@ionashop.com
www.sda-races.com

Scottish Executive
www.scotland.gov.uk

Scottish Independent Hostels
The Secretary
PO Box 7024
Fort William
PH33 6YX
www.hostel-scotland.co.uk

Scottish Natural Heritage
enquiries@snh.co.uk
www.snh.org.uk
(offices throughout Scotland)

Scotways
24 Annandale Street
Edinburgh
EH7 4AN
Tel. 0131 558 1222
info@scotways.com
www.scotways.com

Scottish Youth Hostel Association
SYHA National Office
7 Glebe Crescent
Stirling
FK8 2JA

Tel. 01786 891 400
info@syha.org.uk
reservations@syha.org.uk
www.syha.org.uk

sportscotland
Caledonia House
South Gyle
Edinburgh
EH12 9DQ
Tel. 0131 317 7200
Child.protection@sportsscotland.org.uk
www.sportscotland.org.uk

Visit Scotland
(Tourist information)
www.visitscotland.com

FIRST AID COURSE PROVIDERS

The British Association of Ski Patrollers
20 Lorn Drive
Glencoe
Argyll
Tel. 01855 811 443
www.basp.org.uk

Lagganlia Centre for Outdoor Education
Kincraig
Kingussie
Inverness shire
PH21 1NG
Tel. 01540 651 265

Technical & Safety Services
Peter Leach
9 Elcho Rd
Longniddry
East Lothian
EH32 0LB
Tel 01875 852060

First Aid Training Services
Deemouth Business Centre
South Esplanade East
Aberdeen
AB11 9BP

Outwardly Mobile First Aid
Dave Craig
Tel 01540 673826
www.outwardlymobile.com

PLACES TO RIDE

Forestry Commission
(MTB centres and trails throughout the UK)
www.forestry.gov.uk

The Hub (Café, Bike Hire & Shop)
Glentress Forest
near Peebles
EH45 8NB
Tel. 01721 721736
hubintheforest@aol.com
www.thehubintheforest.co.uk

Laggan Wolftrax
BaseCamp MTB
Strathmashie Forest
Laggan
Newtonmore
Tel. 01528 544 780 / 786
http://pages.123-reg.co.uk/basecamp-627134

7 Stanes Project
Forestry Commission Scotland
55/57 Moffat Road
Dumfries
DG1 1NP
Tel. 01387 272 440
www.7stanes.go.uk

Drumlanrig Castle
(Country Park and Cycle Museum)
Ranger Service
Drumlanrig Castle
Thornhill
Dumfriesshire
DG3 4AQ
Tel. 01848 331 555
www.buccleuch.com

Mountain Biking Wales
www.mbwales.com

Appendix

On the following pages is a selection of forms. Some of them are course requirements, some will be more useful once you have passed your assessment and are working as a Leader.

- SMBLA Logbook
- Route Card
- Accident Report Form
- Emergency Contact List
- Bike Safety Check
- Risk Assessment Form
- Child Protection Checklist
- Consent Form

SMBLA Logbook

To be completed by the **Candidate** prior to training and given to the Course Tutor

Name :

Contact Tel.

Please enter below brief details of your recent mountain bike experience

Ride	Date	Venue (e.g. Glentress Forest)	Duration (hrs)	Terrain e.g. singletrack	Weather
1					
2					
3					
4					
5					
6					
7					
8					
9					
10					
11					
12					
13					
14					

15					
16					
17					
18					
19					
20					

Please give any other relevant experience e.g. outdoor qualifications

Please give the name and contact details of someone who is able to act as a referee for your mountain bike experience

Name		Position
Address		E-mail
		Tel.

SMBLA

Scottish Cycling, The Velodrome, London Road, Edinburgh, EH7 6AD
Tel 0131 652 0187 E-mail smbla@scottishcycling.com www.scottishcycling.com

Route Card

Cumulative Distance (km)	O.S. Map(s):		Intermediate Distance (km)
	Grid ref.	Navigational Feature or Point of Interest	
Start			
End			

Escape / Alternative Route(s):

1.

2.

3.

Date:	Start time:	Expected finishing time:
Base / venue:	Group Leader:	Phone / Mobile no.

Additional Comments (transport details, parking facilities, river crossings, viewpoints, food stops, and other useful info)

ACCIDENT REPORT FORM

1. GROUP DETAILS

CALLERS NAME ....TEL NO. ....
(This information is to be given to the emergency services by the person who has gone for help so the emergency services can contact them).

2. TIME OF ACCIDENT .... DATE ....

3. LOCATION: GRID REF ....

DETAILS OF LOCATION IDENTIFICATION, MARKERS ETC... ....

....

4. WHAT HAPPENED? ....

....

5. WHO IS INJURED?

NAME ....

AGE ....   SEX ....

6. WHAT IS THE INJURY ? ....

....

WHAT TREATMENT HAS BEEN CARRIED OUT ? ....

....

7. HOW MANY ARE IN THE REMAINING PARTY & WHAT IS THEIR CONDITION ?

....

HOW ARE THEY EQUIPPED? ....

8. WEATHER & TERRAIN DETAILS AT SITE if relevant: ....

....

9. ANY OTHER INFORMATION: ....

....

10. YOUR BASE EMERGENCY TEL NO. ....
Complete before departure on your expedition!

EMERGENCY CONTACT LIST

NAME of GROUP MEMBER	NAME of EMERGENCY CONTACT	RELATIONSHIP	PHONE NUMBER(S)
Date(s) of Trip		Base contact	
Leader		Base phone nos.	
Comments			

BIKE SAFETY CHECK LIST

BIKE FEATURE	CONDITION / WHAT TO CHECK FOR	PASS	FAIL	COMMENTS
Front tyre	Good tread; no splits; cracks or holes; properly inflated; valve straight			
Front wheel	True; no broken/missing spokes; good rim			
Front hub	No wobble; turns smoothly; wheel securely fixed			
Front brake	Firmly fixed; correctly adjusted			
Front brake pads	Correctly fitted and aligned; not worn away			
Front brake lever	Comfortable position; firmly fixed; no excessive travel; cable not frayed			
Headset/steering	No wobble; correctly adjusted			
Handlebars	Not distorted; ends protected			
Forks	Appear true and undamaged; suspension forks functioning; no leaks			
Frame	Appears true and undamaged			
Rear brake lever	Comfortable position; firmly fixed; no excessive travel; cable not frayed			
Rear Brake	Firmly fixed; correctly adjusted			
Rear brake pa-s	Correctly fitted and aligned; not worn away			
Rear tyre	Good tread; no splits; cracks or holes; properly inflated; valve straight			
Rear wheel	True; no broken/missing spokes; good rim			
Rear hub	No wobble; turns smoothly; wheel securely fixed			
Bottom bracket	No wobble; turns smoothly; lock rings tight			
Chainset	Straight; firmly fixed; teeth not bent or worn			
Pedals	Complete; turning freely; not bent; firmly fixed			
Cassette	Firmly fixed; teeth not worn			
Chain	Not too worn; not slack; not rusty; lubricated properly			
Gears	Properly adjusted; lubricated sufficiently; cables not frayed			
Saddle	Firmly fixed; correctly positionec; correct height			
Lights (if necessary)	Red rear, white front and suitable for purpose; firmly fixed; working!			
Mudguards and any other attachments	Safely fixed			

SAMPLE RISK ASSESSMENT FORM

Date_____

Reassessment date_____

Leader_____

Signature_____

Start location / venue_____

Hazards		Risk Evaluation		Controlling measures	
Location / Map ref.	Description of Hazard	Potential risk & who might be affected	Risk Rating High//Medium/Low	Control measures to reduce the risk	Assessment of effectiveness or proposed amendment

CHILD PROTECTION CHECKLIST

Information source	Be familiar with and keep a copy of:		
Child Protection Policy	✓		
Code of Conduct	✓		
Parental Consent Form	✓		

	Name	Tel. Nos.	
Main Contact Person			
Child Protection Officer / Co-ordinator			
Other Contacts			
Local Social Work Department			
Police Family Protection Unit			
Children 1st			

PARENTAL CONSENT FORM (Sample)

PARTICIPANT DETAILS	
Name	**Date of Birth**
Address	
Home Tel. No.	
Emergency Contact Tel. No(s).	
Name of Doctor	**Surgery Tel. No.**

I agree to my son/daughter / the above named child in my care taking part in the activities outlined below. I understand that he/she takes part at his/her own risk, and accept that no responsibility for accidents or injury or loss or damage to personal property rests with the supervisory staff, unless proven to be caused by their negligence. I declare that to the best of my knowledge my child is competent and medically fit to participate in the activities as part of a group. I agree that medical treatment will be given if necessary and in case of emergency.

Signature of Parent or Guardian...

Date...

Date(s) of activities	
Start time	**End time**
Meeting / Pick-up point	
Activity venue	
Name of Leader	

NATURE OF ACTIVITIES

Summary risk assessment for these activities attached ☐

Index